A Chronological Study by
Woodrow W. Whidden II

Ellen White on the Humanity of Christ

REVIEW AND HERALD® PUBLISHING ASSOCIATION
HAGERSTOWN, MD 21740

The author assumes full responsibility for the accuracy of all facts and quotations as cited in this book.

This book was
Edited by Gerald Wheeler
Designed by Patricia S. Wegh
Cover design by Helcio Deslandes
Typeset: 11.5/13.5 Goudy

PRINTED IN U.S.A.

01 00 99 98 97   10 9 8 7 6 5 4 3 2 1

R&H Cataloging Service
Whidden, Woodrow W., 1944-
    Ellen White on the humanity of Christ. A
chronological study.

    1. White, Ellen Gould Harmon, 1827-1915—Theology.
2. Jesus Christ—Divinity.   3. Jesus Christ—Humanity.
I. Title.

                    232.8

ISBN 0-8280-1250-4

CONTENTS

ABBREVIATIONS

Ellen White Books and Periodicals:

BC   *The Seventh-day Adventist Bible Commentary* (7 vols.)
BE   *Bible Echo*
CG   *Child Guidance*
ChS   *Christian Service*
COL   *Christ's Object Lessons*
CSW   *Counsels on Sabbath School Work*
CT   *Counsels to Parents, Teachers, and Students*
CWE   *Counsels to Writers and Editors*
DA   *The Desire of Ages*
Ed   *Education*
Ev   *Evangelism*
EW   *Early Writings*
FW   *Faith and Works*
GC   *The Great Controversy*
GCB   *General Conference Bulletin*
HS   *Historical Sketches*
IHP   *In Heavenly Places*
MB   *Thoughts From the Mount of Blessing*
MM   *Medical Ministry*
MR   *Manuscript Releases* (21 vols.)
MS   Manuscript
OHC   *Our High Calling*
PC   Paulson Collection
PP   *Patriarchs and Prophets*
QOD   *Seventh-day Adventists Answer Questions on Doctrine*
RH   *Review and Herald*
SC   *Steps to Christ*
SD   *Sons and Daughters of God*
SG   *Spiritual Gifts* (4 vols.)
SM   *Selected Messages* (3 vols.)
SP   *The Spirit of Prophecy* (4 vols.)
ST   *Signs of the Times*
T   *Testimonies for the Church* (9 vols.)
TMK   *That I May Know Him*
WM   *Welfare Ministry*
YI   *Youth's Instructor*

Preface

This book is a popularized expansion of a couple of lengthy chapters taken from my Ph.D. dissertation ("The Soteriology of Ellen G. White: The Persistent Path to Perfection, 1836-1902" [Drew University, 1989]). I undertook my doctoral study to see if a historical, rather than topical or thematic, approach to Ellen White's unfolding understanding of the doctrine of salvation might shed some additional light on her doctrine of Christian perfection. Obviously, one cannot adequately deal with the subject of perfection in the thought of Ellen White without dealing with the closely related subjects of sin and the humanity of Christ.

I do believe that the reader is entitled to know a bit about how I approached the subject. First of all, I tried to bring together, in chronological sequence, every one of Ellen White's statements on the humanity of Christ. The original study covered only up to 1902, but the present study extends to 1915 (the year of her death).

To be as thorough as possible in securing every relevant statement or reference, I did the following:

1. I personally searched through thousands of pages in both the unpublished and published materials, using the laser disk technology for published material and the computerized index the White Estate has developed for her unpublished works.

2. I combed through the writings of important thinkers (the most prominent being Herbert Douglass, Ralph Larson, Robert J. Wieland,

the authors of *Questions on Doctrine*, Robert W. Olson, and Norman Gulley) looking for any important statements by Ellen White.

3. Then I rummaged through every compilation on the subject that I could lay my hands on.

4. Finally, I sent copies of my compilation out to leading scholars on this subject and asked them to (a) supply any statements that I might have overlooked or unwittingly suppressed, and (b) correct any situations in which I did not cite enough of the context to make the appropriate statement stand on its own without distortion. The latter included asking them to criticize any omissions of important phrases that I might have ignored or suppressed in my use of ellipses.

This compilation then became the basis for the chapters of this present study and appears as Appendix B. I have included it so that the reader can easily check the references and more intelligently (and independently) interact with my interpretations.

The documents that form the basis of my chapter 2 (dealing with Ellen White's understanding of sin) were not gathered in as thorough a way. I do, however, feel that I have retrieved enough of the really important statements to do a reasonably accurate topical portrayal of her position. The documents are listed in no particular order, either chronologically or logically, in Appendix A.

The reader should be alerted to the fact that I have tried, as far as possible, to use the terms and expressions of Ellen White rather than related, but alternative, words. Therefore, there will appear a number of words and phrases in quotation marks that I have lifted from larger statements. The reader can almost always assume that when I am discussing an Ellen White statement and the reference is not explicitly apparent, the word or expressions in quotation marks come from her.

The present volume is a sequel to my first book, entitled *Ellen White on Salvation* (Hagerstown, Md.: Review and Herald Pub. Assn., 1995). My earlier work dealt briefly with the nature of Christ, but its major burden was to trace the larger unfolding of her understanding of justification and perfection in Christian experience. The present work can be logically read as either a sequel or an expanded foundation for the first book.

I send forth this work with the prayer that it will help move forward the present discussions on salvation and the nature of Christ. These discussions, in their current spirit, have been proceeding most actively since the mid-1950s and have often been quite acrimonious and divisive. I have no desire to contribute to the division or the acrimony. Furthermore, though I have dearly held positions on the issues involved, I certainly do not claim to be the final word. I would hope that I would be able to change my mind on any of my own opinions if my partners in this important dialogue present sufficient evidence and sanctified reason.

The present volume goes forth with the hopeful prayer that it might further this discussion and possibly contribute some insights to help bring resolution to the present impasse that seems to dominate discussions on the nature of Christ. May God help us all to exercise charity, humility, and resolution in the pursuit of the truth about Jesus—who is the Truth embodied.

Section 1

The Mystery of Christ's Humanity and Human Sinfulness

CHAPTER ONE

Where Have We Been and How Shall We Proceed?

The unfolding of Ellen White's understanding of the nature of Christ[1] was closely bound up with her view of salvation. In fact, to grasp her teaching on salvation it is absolutely necessary to take into consideration her Christology. This is especially pivotal when it comes to the way she understood the relationship between Christ's human nature and Christian perfection.

The study of the nature of Christ is easily the most difficult and challenging theme we could deal with in the thought of Ellen White. The main reason for this results from the profound depths of the subject itself.

To anyone who has ever made a concerted attempt to do an in-depth study of the nature of Christ, the truthfulness of the following Ellen White statement is all too obvious: "Man cannot define this wonderful *mystery*—the blending of the two natures. . . . It can never be explained" (7BC 904, italics supplied). But we also have the promise that the student who persists will be richly rewarded: "The study of the incarnation of Christ is a fruitful field, which will repay the searcher who digs deep for hidden truth" (7-ABC 443).

A Brief History

Another reason for the difficulty of the subject is its highly controversial history. Ralph Larson has demonstrated that Adventism held a strong consensus on the humanity of Christ until the middle 1950s (see Larson's *The Word Was Made Flesh*). We can clearly term the consensus "post-Fall," that is, Christ had a human nature like that of a person after the fall of Adam. George Knight, however, has shown that there was some rather provocative opposition to the "post-Fall" view of A. T. Jones in the mid-1890s.[2] But the controversy of the 1890s was only a briefly noted harbinger of the divisive debate that would begin in the mid-1950s.

The major cause of the outbreak of renewed debate was the publication of the book *Seventh-day Adventists Answer Questions on Doctrine* in 1957. The controversy has continued unabated since then, and the church has not yet reached a satisfactory consensus on the topic. The major figure in all this seems to be the late M. L. Andreasen.[3]

Andreasen had had a long and productive career as a much-respected minister, writer, and teacher.[4] But the position taken on the humanity of Christ in *Questions on Doctrine* provoked him to a most strenuous reaction—even leading to his being disfellowshipped. In the years since 1957 Andreasen has had his strong admirers and stout opponents, and such reactions have precipitated the lengthy and acrimonious debate that continues to the present. The contending camps have been rather easily identified as the "pre-Fall" and the "post-Fall" groups.

The post-Fall advocates[5] hold that Jesus had a nature like ours, and His likeness to us is absolutely essential to our own victory over sin. In other words, since He was victorious in a nature just like ours, we can also have perfect victory over sin. The post-Fall partisans are quick to claim that any such perfections are the results of the Spirit imparting God's grace to the faithful. Many advocates of the "post-Fall" view, following in the wake of Andreasen, also hold that the perfect victory gained by the "final generation" is absolutely essential to the vindication of God and the ushering in of the second coming of Jesus.

The pre-Fall partisans emphasize that while Jesus possessed the fullness of humanity, that humanity was at the same time sinless. Such sinlessness involves not only the absence of acts of sin, but also any inherent depravity or innate propensities and tendencies to sin. Pre-Fall advocates tend to want to lay more emphasis on Jesus' role as justifying substitute than they do on His example for the overcomer. Furthermore, they want to distinguish sinful acts from sinful nature. While both sides speak of victory over sin through faith in the grace of Christ, the pre-Fall writers want to qualify more carefully the perfection that the faithful can achieve through grace.[6]

Probably the majority of current academics and ministers hold to some version of the pre-Fall view. Where the majority of laypersons stand is not entirely clear. But at least a strong minority (both lay and ministerial) in the church care deeply about the issue and are willing to take forthright stands for the post-Fall position. Furthermore, the post-Fall people feel that their teachings are extremely vital to the spiritual health and mission of the church. In fact, they seem to want to elevate their position to the status of a "pillar" or "landmark" testing truth that will help to clearly define what I have called "essential" Adventism.[7]

The Basic Issue

Let's try to grasp the issue at its very core. The more traditional post-Fall interpreters have tended to read Ellen White as emphasizing the *similarities*, seeing Christ as sinful in nature (though not in action), while the seeming majority of more recent interpreters are pre-Fall and have emphasized the *differences* between His nature and ours. Their accent falls on the *uniqueness* of the sinlessness of His nature and life.

Ellen White aptly states her basic proposition in the following quotation: "Christ reaches us where we are. He took our nature and overcame, that we through taking His nature might overcome. Made 'in the likeness of sinful flesh' (Rom. 8:3), He lived a sinless life" (DA 311, 312). The *key question* for our study is: *In the thought of Ellen White, just how much like our sinful human nature is the human nature of Christ?*

Eric C. Webster is certainly correct when he reminds us that "almost every area of belief is influenced by one's departure point regarding the nature of Christ" (Webster 50). This is especially true of such important salvation issues as justification, sanctification, the atonement, the purpose of the great controversy theme, and the nature of sin.

Other Complicating Factors

In addition to its mystery and its controverted history, three other factors make this subject especially challenging: (1) the sheer bulk of Ellen White's writings and (2) her lack of a systematic treatment of the subject in any particular article or book. These difficulties are further complicated by (3) numerous complex statements that give her Christology a very intricate balance or tension between pre-Fall sinless *uniqueness* and post-Fall *identity* with our "sinful nature."

Depth, controversy, and complexity notwithstanding, we should not let anything deter us in this important quest for understanding. The issue is too central simply to ignore.

So I encourage the reader to approach it patiently, but also prayerfully and respectfully, remembering "to heed the words spoken by Christ to Moses at the burning bush, 'Put off thy shoes from off thy feet, for the place where on thou standest is holy ground'" (QOD 647). Truth is then best served if we take off our argumentative, opinionated "shoes" and come "with the humility of a learner, with a contrite heart" (*ibid.*).

Deity and the Trinity

While the major burden of this book is the humanity of Christ, we should devote a few preliminary lines to Ellen White's understanding of His deity. All discussions of Christ's humanity would be without any real point if we did not also see Him as fully divine. He is truly the unique God-man!

Ellen White was decisively a believer in the full deity of Christ. We can characterize her as Trinitarian in her convictions, even from her earliest years (7-ABC 437-442; Ev 613-617).

What is truly remarkable about her Trinitarian views is that she held them despite the strong Arian influences in nineteenth-century Seventh-day Adventism, especially among many of the leading ministers. Arianism[8] is an ancient heresy that denies that Jesus has existed co-eternally with God the Father. It teaches that there was a time when Christ was not.

Furthermore, it is of some interest to note that these anti-Trinitarian ministers included none other than her own husband. James White came from the Christian Connection Church, which had strong Arian tendencies, and some of his early statements revealed an anti-Trinitarian bias (Webster 34).

But in spite of these strong influences, Ellen White went on her own independent way, quite willing to go against the strong Arianism of the Adventist ministers of her time (*ibid.* 72).

She never attacked or directly corrected any of these persons for their Arian views, but she became increasingly explicit in her own forthright declarations of the full deity of Christ and clear affirmations of the Trinity.

For the purposes of this study, we need to state clearly that by the time of the 1888 Minneapolis General Conference session Ellen White was forcefully affirming the full, eternal deity of Christ.

What Terminology Shall We Use?
"Pre-Fall" or "Post-Fall"?

Before we begin our study of Ellen White's unfolding understanding of Christ's humanity, we need some further clarification on terminology. I am suggesting that we lay aside the expressions "pre-Fall" and "post-Fall" in this discussion. The reason for this suggestion is twofold.

First of all, they are not very helpful, in that Jesus was neither completely pre-Fall nor post-Fall—as such terms would imply. On the one hand, He was pre-Fall in the sense that His humanity was not "infected" with sinful, corrupt tendencies, or propensities to sin, such as we are born with. On the other hand, He was post-Fall in the sense that His humanity was "affected" by sin, in which He never indulged.

Thus He was neither completely one nor the other. In a very important sense He was both, and the all-or-nothing implications of such expressions are not helpful.

Second, the expressions have become so freighted with controversial overtones that some new terminology, more reflective of the rich tension and balance residing in Ellen White's thought, might prove helpful.

"Identity" and "Uniqueness"

I am suggesting the terms *identity* and *uniqueness*. The *identity* expressions speak to Jesus' profound similarities to human beings with their sinful natures, while the *uniqueness* expressions point to the sinlessness of His humanity. For Jesus really to be able to identify with us, He needed to be one with us. To be our sinless, effectual substitute, He needed to be clearly unique and distinguished from us—not just in actions, but also in nature! It is not one or the other, but both that are absolutely essential to His effectual work as a complete Saviour.

Objectives of This Study

Our main initial objective is to shed light on the lingering debate over the nature of Christ by seeking to demonstrate how Ellen White's understanding unfolded in her ministry before and after 1888. But the ultimate objective is to clarify how her grasp of the nature of Christ influenced her teachings on salvation, especially in the critical years following 1888.

Sections 2 and 3, dealing with the historical developments, will then be followed by Section 4, in which I will lay out my own understanding of the humanity of Christ and its implications for salvation and the atonement. And finally I include a response to my interpretation as well as my reply to it. In a sincere attempt to initiate a new dialogue with the "post-Fall" advocates, I requested written responses (for the expressed purpose of publication in this book) from Herbert Douglass, Ralph Larson, Robert Wieland, Dennis Priebe, and Kevin Paulson. Paulson, a self-proclaimed "historic Adventist," was the only one to tender a response. Herbert Douglass and Dennis Priebe were unable to do so because of the press of other responsibilities. Ralph Larson and Robert Wieland pointedly declined my invitation for other reasons. I do believe that Paulson's spirited response (and my brief reply) will help to clarify the central issues in the debate over the humanity of Christ.

The entire work will then finish with three appendixes that include (1) a collection of statements from Ellen White on "sin" and sinful nature (Appendix A), (2) a rather extensive collection of all the important, essential statements that she made on the humanity of Christ (Appendix B), and (3) a brief treatment of the recently discovered Kellogg letter of 1903 (Appendix C). Because of the developmental nature of this study, I have listed the collection of statements dealing with the humanity of Christ in chronological order.

It is hoped that the appendixes (especially A and B) will enable the reader to come to a more intelligent response to my interpretations and a fuller understanding of the breadth and depth of Ellen White's thinking on these subjects. I do not claim to be the last word, and therefore I put forth these collections to help facilitate the reader's prayerful, careful, and independent reflection.

But before we begin our review of the way her understanding of Christ's humanity unfolded, one other important preliminary consideration cries out for attention: What did Ellen White mean when she used the expressions "sin" and "sinful nature"? It is to this important issue that we now turn our attention.

---

[1] Theologians refer to the doctrine of the person and nature of Christ as Christology.

[2] See Knight's interesting discussion in the chapter "The Nature of Christ," pp. 132-150 in his *From 1888 to Apostasy*.

[3] For an excellent overview of Andreasen's thinking, see Roy Adams's *The Sanctuary Doctrine*, pp. 165-230, with special attention to pp. 202-230.

[4] Virginia Steinweg has sympathetically traced Andreasen's life in her *Without Fear or Favor*.

[5] The major published proponents of this position are Herbert Douglass (and probably the editorial leadership of the *Review* in the 1970s), Robert J. Wieland, Thomas Davis, C. Mervyn Maxwell, and Ralph Larson. Dissidents such as the early Robert Brinsmead in his "Sanctuary Awakening" movement and the current "independent" ministries have also strongly advocated it. What seems to be the common thread of all the post-Fall advocates has been their admiration for and indebtedness to M. L. Andreasen.

[6] The major published proponents of this position have been the anonymous authors of *Questions on Doctrine* (most probably R. A. Anderson, Leroy E. Froom, and W. E. Read), Edward (Ted) Heppenstall, Hans K. LaRondelle, Raoul Dederen, Desmond Ford, and Norman Gulley.

[7] Such issues will be explored in chapter 10.

[8] This teaching was given its classic expression by and is named after Arius, a third-century theologian from Alexandria, Egypt.

CHAPTER TWO

What Is Sin?

The question of just how much Jesus can be like sinful humanity (both lost and redeemed) and still be a Saviour for them is crucial as to where we will end up in our understanding of Christ's humanity.

Let's try to get a grip on this issue by posing some more questions: Is there something unique to sinful human nature that makes it tragically different when compared with the human nature of Christ? Is there something special about the human nature of Christ that makes it redemptively different when compared with our own sinful natures? What does Ellen White mean by the word "sin"? Does it apply only to acts, or does it also cover a deeply deranging condition that predisposes to sin? Could Jesus be our Saviour if He had such a deeply deranged condition? And finally, did Ellen White address such questions? In answer to the last question, we can clearly state that she did. It is hoped that her answers to the previous questions will also become clear.

Sin, the Human Condition, and Salvation

Ellen White defined sin as both acts of transgressing the law of God (1SM 320)[1] and a condition of depravity that involves "inherent" sinful "propensities," "inclinations," "tendencies," and a "bent" to sin (i.e., inbred or indwelling sin) (5BC 1128, Ed 29, IHP 195).

A quick glance at Appendix A in this volume should immediately alert us to the fact that Ellen White very clearly taught that sin was more than evil actions contrary to the law of God. Sin certainly involves such acts, but she recognized a more profound and pervasive syndrome called depravity. It is a terribly systemic sickness, a deep-seated infection that produces all sorts of tragic symptoms. The symptoms (wrong acts, evil words, hateful attitudes, and so on) are only the tip of the iceberg called human depravity.

Depravity, Guilt, and Original Sin

Though Ellen White has a clearly stated understanding of infectious depravity, we still must move very carefully in this area. We need to take such deliberate care in accurately expressing her teaching simply because she is hard to categorize in the classic ways that theologians have normally characterized teachings on depravity.

She was certainly not in the Augustinian/Calvinistic tradition of total depravity. Augustine and his admirers (especially in the Calvinistic tradition) considered humans to be so depraved by "original sin" that they were totally unable to choose their eternal destiny. God had to irresistibly elect who was to be saved and who was to be damned. This quite obviously does not fit the thinking of Ellen White.

She was clearly in what we call the Arminian[2] or free-will tradition: that is, humans, empowered by the grace of God, were viewed as free to choose. But at the same time Ellen White also explicitly states the reality of sinful depravity and corruption in her writings dealing with the human condition. She clearly spoke of depravity as the natural condition of humans: "We must remember that our hearts are naturally depraved, and we are unable of ourselves to pursue a right course" (IHP 163; cf. 195 and see CT 544).

What seems to concern most Seventh-day Adventists in any discussion of sin is the issue of guilt, especially when someone employs the venerated but theologically loaded expression "original sin." The question is often posed this way: Do we inherit guilt from Adam simply because we are his genetic and spiritual heirs? Are we condemned by God to an eternal death just because God allowed us to come into the world "born in sin"—that is to say, in a sinful condition?

In answer to these questions, the thought of Ellen White has some complex aspects that should signal caution in the way we seek to express her response.

She was forthright in declaring that Adam's sin definitely caused his "posterity" to be "born with inherent propensities of disobedience" (5BC 1128). But such expressions as "original sin" (with its Augustinian/Calvinistic overtones) do not quite seem to fit her thinking. On the other hand, the idea that humans come into the world morally neutral (with no natural tendencies one way or the other) or as basically good does not seem to square with her views of sin.[3]

When we try to come to terms with her understanding of original sin, it seems that she closely approaches the views of the great Arminian preacher John Wesley. Wesley certainly viewed sinners as depraved to the extent that they have no ability to originate a saving experience. But he did not see them as so depraved that they had to be totally subject to a deterministic election on the part of the redeeming God. Sinners are not free to initiate a saving experience, but they are free to accept or reject it. This probably sums up Ellen White's understanding also.

She used "original sin" only once: "At its very source human nature was corrupted. And ever since then sin has continued its hateful work, reaching from mind to mind. Every sin committed awakens echoes of the original sin" (RH, Apr. 16, 1901; cf. 5T 645). Here she was clear that Adam's original sin echoes itself in the corruption of human nature.

Again we must state that the part of her thought that is hardest to characterize is not "corruption," "depravity," or "tendencies" ("propensities" and a "bent") to sin, but the issue of guilt.

John Wood has flatly declared that she "rejects the doctrine of original sin" (The Sanctuary and the Atonement 716). Wood, however, is possibly a bit too dogmatic when he declares that "it is a fallen nature, with hereditary tendencies to sin, rather than original guilt, that makes a 'sinner'" (ibid.). What, then, are we to make of the following Ellen White statement? "The inheritance of children is that of sin. . . . As related to the first Adam, men receive from him nothing but guilt and the sentence of death" (CG 475). The passage caused Robert Olson to declare that "we are born in a state of guilt inherited from Adam" ("Outline Studies" 28).

The reader may reasonably question what Ellen White meant when she declared that "men receive from him nothing but guilt."

The best conclusion seems to be that she understood the issue practically rather than theoretically. She was very clear that "selfishness is inwrought in our very being" and that "it has come to us as an inheritance" (HS 138, 139). The central issue, however, was not so much Adam's guilt as it was individual guilt that arises from particular sinful choices.

In another setting she made this down-to-earth, commonsense observation: "It is inevitable that children should suffer from the consequences of parental wrongdoing, but they are not punished for the parents' guilt, except as they participate in their sins" (PP 306). The inevitability was then expressed with the realistic observation that "it is usually the case, however, that children walk in the steps of their parents" (ibid.). "As a result of Adam's disobedience every human being is a transgressor of the law, sold under sin" (IHP 146).

Ellen White simply did not feel moved to address the question of the fairness of God in allowing a sinful nature to be passed on to Adam's posterity.[4] The thought that God allows humans to be subject to an inheritance that leads inevitably to sinful acts, which result in guilt, simply did not disturb her.

For the servant of the Lord, the issue was a matter of practical realism: humans have "sinful natures," "a bent to evil," "propensities to sin," etc., that lead to sin and guilt. Because of this, sinful humans are responsible before God to do something about their blameworthy condition.

This we see further evidenced in her understanding that babies did not need to be baptized (christened) and that they could be saved, even though they had unsaved parents (2SM 258-260).

How is it, then, that sinful beings can be blameworthy and yet not be bearing such sin as will land them in hell? The answer that seems implicit (but not totally explicit) in her writings appears to go something like this: whatever guilt infants (or any other person lacking ability to understand God's redemptive will) may have incurred (because of the presence of sinful natures in their souls) was most likely understood to have been implicitly cared for by the saving provisions of the death of Jesus as their sin-bearer. Again we must emphasize that she does not totally spell it out, but the implication draws very close to being explicit.

She made the following statement in a letter to a family mourning the death of their children who had been lost at sea: "This we know, that His love is greater than ours possibly can be, and Jesus so loved them that He gave His life to redeem them" (ibid. 261). What is somewhat unclear about this statement is that we don't know the ages and salvation experiences of the children. It seems they were not infants.

In another statement, however, she makes it clear that infants will be in heaven, including those whose mothers didn't make it. "As the little infants come forth immortal from their dusty beds, they immediately wing their way to their mother's arms. They meet again nevermore to part. But many of the little ones have no mother there. We listen in vain for the rapturous song of triumph from the mother. The angels receive the motherless infants and conduct them to the tree of life" (ibid. 260). Thus Ellen White was quite explicit that the death of Christ has saving efficiency for infants, even though they cannot choose to be saved.

Robert Olson concurs: "We inherit guilt from Adam so that even a baby that dies a day after birth needs a Saviour though the child never committed a sin of its own" ("Outline Studies" 28).

"Their entrance into the kingdom is based entirely on the merits of Jesus" (ibid.).

Human Depravity and Christ's Saving Merit

Now the reader is probably saying, "What does all this have to do with the nature of Christ?" Again let us pose the question central to this study: Could Jesus have the very same nature that we receive from Adam and still be our Saviour? I would suggest that the best initial answer to our question would be to pose another set of questions: Could Jesus still be our saving, sacrificial substitute and still be called "depraved," "corrupt," and be characterized as having natural propensities and tendencies to sin—"bent to evil"? Could Jesus save babies born with an "inheritance" of "selfishness . . . inwrought in" their "very being" if He had been born with the same "inheritance" of "selfishness" (HS 138, 139)? For Ellen White, the answer would appear to be a firm no!

Such a conclusion seems to find further support in a very powerful theme arising out of her clear vision of Christ as the believers' constantly interceding high priest. The thought goes like this: Human sinfulness makes even the best efforts of penitent, redeemed believers meritoriously unacceptable. Only the intercessory work of Christ as He perfumes the believers' good works with the merits of His own blood can counteract this fact!

This theme reveals the compellingly practical side of Ellen White's thinking on salvation and the humanity of Christ: "Oh, that all may see that everything in obedience, in penitence, in praise and thanksgiving, must be placed upon the glowing fire of the righteousness of Christ" (1SM 344). We should carefully note that in this important statement she was clearly referring to "the religious services, the prayers, the praise, the penitent confession of sin" that "ascend from *true believers* . . . to the heavenly sanctuary, . . . but passing through the corrupt channels of humanity, they are so defiled that unless purified by blood, they can never be of value with God" (*ibid.*; italics supplied).[5]

The Implications for Christ's Humanity

It appears to me that the implications of this provocative statement in *Selected Messages* (book 1, p. 344) are rather compelling! Once again it seems more forceful to focus on them through a question: Could Jesus have a nature just like ours (with "corrupt channels") and still be our interceding advocate and high priest?

At this juncture of our study I will not venture a full-blown interpretation of the issue of Jesus and sin. But as we bring this chapter to a close, I would appeal to the reader to keep these questions in mind as we commence our review of the unfolding of Ellen White's understanding of the humanity of Christ.

---

[1] In regard to her defining sin as the transgression of the law, it is clear that she understood the will of God to involve many revealed particulars. It must be emphasized, however, that the essence of all lawful requirement was expressed in the Ten Commandments.

[2] "Arminian" comes from the late-sixteenth-century Dutch Calvinist theologian Jacobus Arminius, who reacted against the very deterministic trends of the Calvinistic tradition. The most famous popularizer of Arminian concepts was John Wesley.

[3] We often refer to such a view as Pelagianism, named after a British monk (Pelagius) who was a contemporary of Augustine of Hippo. He held that humans are not naturally corrupt and fallen and that they have the natural ability to do the right thing—if they so choose.

[4] Edward Heppenstall, the most influential Seventh-day Adventist theologian of this generation, has some challenging concepts about the way "sinful nature" is passed along, especially as it relates to the sinlessness of the humanity of Christ. See *The Man Who Is God*, pp. 107-150.

[5] This statement was the capsheaf of a lengthy development of this theme in Ellen White's thought. For a similar type of statement, note the following from her important manuscript 36, 1890: "All [that "duty prescribes"] must be laid upon the fire of Christ's righteousness to cleanse it from its earthly odor before it rises in a cloud of fragrant incense to the great Jehovah and is accepted as a sweet savor. . . .

"If you would gather together everything that is good and holy and noble and lovely in man and then present the subject to the angels of God as acting a part in the salvation of the human soul or in merit, the proposition would be rejected as treason. . . .

"And any works that man can render to God will be far less than nothingness. My requests are made acceptable only because they are laid upon Christ's righteousness" (cited in FW 23, 24).

Depravity always leaves the stench of "earthly odor" on even the best that believers can produce. This stench makes such "works" meritoriously unacceptable.

Section 2

DEVELOPMENTS
BEFORE 1888

CHAPTER THREE

The Humanity
of Christ Before 1888
Part 1

W e will deal here with only the major expressions and important, pathbreaking statements of the pre-1888 era. We could cite many more,[1] but these examples should be sufficient to help us grasp Ellen White's understanding as she approached Minneapolis and its watershed crisis.

Early Significant Statements

The first significant theological statement regarding the humanity of Christ does not come until 1858, when she clearly spoke of Him as taking "man's fallen nature" (1SG 25).[2] She employed this expression regularly during the balance of her prophetic career.

In 1863 she declared that He "knows our infirmities," but she was clear to qualify "infirmities" as not involving "sin" (RH, Jan. 20, 1863). The expression "infirmities" was one of her favorites. In fact, "infirmities," "fallen nature," and "weakness(es)" (or "weakened") were far and away her most preferred ways of describing Christ's *identity* with humanity.

In 1869 she made the following statement that so richly expresses her profoundly tensioned balance between *identity* and *uniqueness*: "He is a brother in our infirmities, but not in possessing like passions. As the sinless One, His nature recoiled from evil" (2T 202). Christ is infirm, and yet His passions are distinctly different from ours as His nature was "sinless," since it "recoiled from evil."

A Key Issue in Terminology

Our discussion really cannot proceed further without some clarification of Ellen White's intended meaning when she used such words as "sinless" and "sinful." As we discuss the humanity of Christ, we must address issues of terminology with some care. If we are not relatively precise in our usage, we might just be talking past one another in our search for consensus.

Ralph Larson, a well-known writer on the issue of Ellen White's Christology, has tried to resolve the issue of what she taught about the humanity of Christ by making some rather forced and strained distinctions between nominal, adjectival, and adverbial usages of such expressions as "sinful" and "sinless" (Larson 16, 17).

Note carefully Larson's claim about the adjectival form "sinful": "Ellen White consistently uses this term, *sinful,* to describe the flesh (nature) in which Christ made His earthly tabernacle. She saw His flesh (nature) as having the same tendencies (*natural* propensities, not *evil* propensities) that our flesh (nature) has" (*ibid.* 16).

He contends, however, that the word "sinfulness" has the meaning of *"a state of being."* "This is far beyond *a tendency toward.* It must involve the actual practice of sinning. Ellen White applies this term to humans, but *never* to Christ, lest she be understood as saying that Christ sinned. . . . She did not equate *sinful* with *sinfulness*" (*ibid.*).

Larson takes the same tack with the word "sinless" by declaring that she "applies the term *sinlessness* to the human nature of Christ, but not the term *sinless*" (*ibid.* 17; italics supplied).

What are we to make of Larson's interpretations?

The first thing we must note about his suggestions is a lack of consistency. One would think that there would be some sort of consistent pattern in the use of adjective and noun versions of the same word. But in one place he claims that the noun "sinfulness" cannot apply to Christ, but when it comes to the noun "sinlessness," it can be. It is immediately apparent that such arbitrary applications should alert us to the forced, artificial nature of his method of doing theology by "dictionary."

Any dictionary will say that "sinless" is only the adjectival form of the noun "sinlessness," and "sinlessly" is the adverbial form. One is not comparing "sinless" apples with "sinful" oranges, but the different uses to which the "sin" apple is put.

We must carefully consider each word in its context to discern its meaning and usage in any given setting. It is clear that the nominal, adjectival, or adverbial forms do not make that much difference in the thinking of Ellen White (or, for that matter, any English-speaking person's use of the variations of the word "sin").

Also, we must candidly point out that Larson's contention that Ellen White does not apply "sinless" to the human nature of Christ is simply not supported by the following clear-cut evidence: "Christ is a perfect representation of God on the one hand, and a perfect specimen of *sinless humanity* on the other hand" (7BC 907; italics supplied).

Important Statements in 1872

The year 1872 witnessed some very important comments by Ellen White that further clarified her understanding of Jesus' sinless *uniqueness*. She made it clear that "man could not atone for man," as "his sinful, fallen condition would constitute him an imperfect offering" (RH, Dec. 17, 1872). This indicated that whatever she meant by the expression "fallen nature" or "condition," when applied to Christ, was essentially different for Him than it was when used to describe "sinful, fallen" human beings. Otherwise, any human who performed sinlessly could be a possible Saviour.

But sinless perfection, even that which was Adam's before the Fall, was not the only requirement to be a Saviour. She went on to state that "there could be no sacrifice acceptable to God for him [fallen human beings], unless the offering made should in value be superior to man as he was in his state of perfection and innocency.

"The divine Son of God was the only sacrifice of sufficient value to fully satisfy the claims of God's perfect law."

She thus declared Christ to be "perfect, and undefiled by sin" (*ibid.*).

We should note that the passage was her first definite discussion of the humanity of Christ in relationship to His role as a sinless, justifying substitute. It is clear that humans could not produce an obedience that had saving merit. The meritorious deficiency in human obedience was because of not only their "sinful, fallen condition," but also their humanity itself—as "there could be no sacrifice acceptable to God for him, unless the offering made should in value *be superior* to man as he was in his state of perfection and innocency" (*ibid.*; italics supplied).

In the thought of Ellen White a valid, saving sacrifice required not only the sinlessness of Christ's human nature and character, but also divinity.

This year, 1872, also marked the first use of another expression of Christ's *identity* with sinful humans: the famous phrase of Romans 8:3— "in the likeness of sinful flesh" (RH, Dec. 24, 1872). She employed this terminology quite frequently during the following years, with the most numerous usages coming in 1895 and 1896. But her most profound expression of *identity* would come two years later. It is to this important and foundational statement that we now turn attention.

---

1 The reader is encouraged to consult Appendix B at the end of this book.

2 For Ellen White, "nature" usually refers to a person's inheritance, or what he or she is "naturally" born with. "Character" refers more to what a person develops either because of, or in spite of, his or her natural inheritance.

CHAPTER FOUR

The Humanity of Christ Before 1888 Part 2

Ellen White's Most Profound Statement of "Identity"

Mid-1874 witnessed the most comprehensive and foundational statement that Ellen White would ever make on the deep *identity* of Christ with sinful humanity. Appearing in the *Review* of July 28, it would be paraphrased or directly quoted in numerous successive works over the next 28 years (see especially DA 117).

Clearly contrasting Christ's condition during His earthly life with Adam's before the Fall, she declared Him not to be "in as favorable a position in the desolate wilderness to endure the temptations of Satan as was Adam when he was tempted in Eden." Jesus "humbled Himself and took man's nature after the race had wandered four thousand years from Eden, and from their original state of purity and uprightness." "Man's nature" that Christ took at this time she declared to be terribly marked with "physical, mental, and moral degeneracy."

In succeeding paragraphs she gave further details:

"The human family had been departing every successive generation, farther from the original purity, wisdom, and knowledge which Adam possessed in Eden." She saw Christ as having to bear "the sins and infirmities of the race as they existed when He came to the earth" so that with "the weaknesses of fallen man upon Him, He was to stand the temptations of Satan upon all points wherewith man would be assailed. . . . Adam . . .

the perfection of manhood" was contrasted with "the second Adam," who had entered the human race after it "had been decreasing in size and physical strength, and sinking lower in the scale of moral worth. . . . He took human nature, and bore the infirmities and degeneracy of the race."

The most striking expressions in this pathbreaking article had to do with the very strong implication that Christ took human nature without the "original state of purity and uprightness" of Adam before the Fall, and that His human nature was marked by "moral degeneracy" and beset with "infirmities and degeneracy" that had sunk "lower in the scale of moral worth."

The meaning of Ellen White's rather startling expressions is somewhat elusive, but the essence of it seems to be something like this: Christ had a human nature with a lessened capacity (He was *affected* by sin), yet it was a capacity that still was not *infected* with natural tendencies or propensities to sin.

An illustration from the world of sports might prove helpful. In 1993 basketball superstar Michael Jordan "retired" for almost two years. Near the end of the 1995 NBA season he came back to play. But great as Jordan was (and still is), it was evident that the retirement period had caused some "degeneracy" to his prodigious skills. I think one could safely say that the athletic propensities or natural instincts were still there, but the energy and timing (by Jordan's own admittance) had been eroded. And even though he has made a spectacular comeback in the 1996 season, there will certainly come a time when even the great Jordan will fall "lower" in the scale of athletic "worth." The old "propensities," "tendencies," and instincts will still be there, but he will simply not have the energy, strength, and timing that enabled him to dominate his sport. If for no other reason, age alone will ultimately affect Jordan's performance, but it will never erode his basic basketball "propensities."

I suggest this initial (and tentative) interpretation on the basis of all that Ellen White had to say on Christ's humanity. Although I realize that my conclusions might be a bit premature, I do ask that the readers (especially those with post-Fall sympathies) patiently hear me out on all of the evidence yet to be presented.

Was Christ "Infected With" or "Affected by" Sin?

We need to pause here to make a further crucial point about interpretative terminology. I am here employing *infected* in the sense of a degenerative disease and consciously use it in contrast to *affected*, which I use to denote the sense of an inflicted injury. Quite a difference exists between having AIDS and being afflicted with ("affected by") a broken arm. Christ was broken by sin (*ours only*), but "His spiritual nature" was never infected with its viral "taint" (7BC 449).

The Significance of the *Review* Article of 1874

Whatever these striking expressions of the *Review* article of 1874 meant, they certainly heightened Ellen White's profoundly balanced tension between Christ's redemptive necessity to retain both a fallen nature and sinlessness. It certainly tipped the balance toward the fallen side, and the fact that she often reached back in succeeding years to draw on this statement in other important writings on Christ's humanity accents the foundational importance of this commentary on Christ's *identity* with sinful humanity.

Developments During the Rest of the Pre-1888 Era
No Dependence on His Own Divine Power

Early in 1875 Ellen White gave the first of many declarations that Christ, in His battle with temptation, did not depend on His innately divine power, an important expression of His *identity* with us: "If Christ . . . had exercised His miraculous power to relieve Himself from difficulty, He would have broken the contract made with His Father, to be a probationer in behalf of the race" (RH, Apr. 1, 1875).

This concept of Christ not resorting to His deity to resist Satan's temptations became one of the great themes of her reflections and appeals concerning the meaning of Christ's human nature.

She further developed this theme in the same article with the following stunning statement: "It was as difficult for Him to keep the level of humanity as it is for men to rise above the low level of their depraved natures, and be partakers of the divine nature."

Temptation Heightened by the Superiority of His Character

The year 1877 saw the publication of volume 2 of *The Spirit of Prophecy*, which contained a most significant statement. While Ellen White spoke of Christ taking "upon Himself the form and nature of fallen man" (39), she emphasized Christ's *uniqueness* in comparison with "man" by stating that "every enticement to evil, which men find so difficult to resist, was brought to bear upon the Son of God in as much greater degree as His character was superior to that of fallen man" (88).

She would often repeat the essence of this thought. She expressed it usually in terms of "character," but at least twice in terms of "nature." Note her usage in 1888:

"Christ was not insensible to ignominy and disgrace. . . . He felt it as much more deeply and acutely than we can feel suffering, as His nature was more exalted, and pure, and holy than that of the sinful race for whom He suffered" (RH, Sept. 11, 1888).

Here she clearly declared Christ to have had a more exalted nature than the race for which He suffered. As pointed out previously, whether expressed in terms of His character or His nature, she declared Him to be "more exalted, and pure, and holy than . . . the sinful race for whom He suffered." Thus the "greater degree" of His purity of character and nature made sin and temptation that much more "difficult to resist."

This concept of the power and suffering of temptation being in proportion to the purity and holiness of character and nature is a bit elusive. But the gist of it seems to be along the following lines: Though Christ had a sinless and pure nature (in contrast to "fallen man"), His sinlessness was of no advantage to Him in His struggles with the temptations and enticements of the devil, but only made His contact with sin more "unspeakably painful."

"There Was No Sin in Him"

In the *Review* of May 27, 1884, Ellen White made an interesting contrast between Christ and humanity: "There was no sin in Him that Satan could triumph over, no weakness or defect that he could use to his advantage. But we are sinful by nature, and we have a work to do to cleanse the soul-temple of every defilement." The expression "no sin in Him" strongly implies a sinless nature, especially when seen in contrast to humans, whom she understood to be "sinful by nature."

The Pre-1888 Summation

By October of the critical year 1888, Ellen White had clearly stated her understanding of the humanity of Christ in a powerfully balanced tension that emphasized the profound *identity* of His full and real humanity with "fallen man" and His *unique* sinlessness as "fallen man's" fully effective, saving sacrifice. While she mainly focused on the meaning of Christ's humanity to sanctification and character change, she also referred to the implications of His sinless nature and life for pardon through the justifying merits of His substitutionary death.

Section 3

DEVELOPMENTS
AFTER 1888

CHAPTER FIVE

The Humanity of Christ and Salvation After 1888: Part I: The Years 1889-1895

I n this chapter and the next we will give an overview of important statements in Ellen White's unfolding understanding of the nature of Christ and the ways she employed them during the most important period of her expositions on issues related to salvation (the six years following the Minneapolis General Conference session).

What is rather shocking about the formation of her perspective is that she made no really striking or pathbreaking developments in her teaching on Christology during this crucial period. I refer to this lack of development as shocking in the sense that there has been so much debate about the impact of her Christology on her teachings about salvation.

The simple fact is that further developments in her understanding of Christ's humanity played no markedly significant role in her great emphasis on justification and sanctification in the years following 1888.

The reader might therefore wonder why we even need these chapters. I would suggest two reasons for the following study:

1. Further attention will help clarify her usage of Christ's humanity in her powerful initiative to emphasize the centrality and primacy of a balanced presentation on salvation.

2. An examination of her most important statements will confirm that the post-1888 statements on the nature of Christ were only further elaborations of what she had already clearly stated before 1888. I do this very consciously in light of the claims of those individuals who have tried

to convince us that Christology was one of the central issues involved in Ellen White's great emphasis on salvation coming out of the Minneapolis General Conference session. In fact, I invite the reader to carefully go through *The Ellen G. White 1888 Materials*. What you will discover is that she has little to say about Christology (in the sense of technical theological discourse) in all her comments on Minneapolis and its aftermath.

Christology is most certainly always at the base of Ellen White's teachings on salvation, but serious theological emphasis on the nature of Christ (both His deity and humanity) was not the major salvation feature that fed into or arose out of the Minneapolis crisis.

Developments From 1889 to 1895

About the only notable impact that Ellen White's unfolding understanding of the nature of Christ made on her great presentations about salvation after 1888 occurs in the following theme: She vigorously presented Christ's nature as a mysterious blending, or union, of humanity and deity, a blending deemed essential to Christ's uniquely saving work. In other words, this significant development arises more out of a sharpening emphasis on the significance of His deity than of just His humanity! This development is nothing new, but the emphasis placed upon it certainly sharpens (cf. above, page 31).

In a sermon given on June 19, 1889 (7BC 904), she proclaimed that "Christ could have done nothing during His earthly ministry in saving fallen man if the divine had not been blended with the human." She further stated that "man cannot define this wonderful mystery—the blending of the two natures. . . . It can never be explained." This declaration that a union of humanity and deity was essential to the atonement became a frequently repeated theme for the balance of her ministry.

It should come as no surprise to us that this theme emphasized the importance of His deity and His sinless humanity as essential to His role as justifying Saviour. Only Jesus "could have paid the penalty of sin" and borne "the sins of every sinner; for all transgressions were imputed unto Him" (RH, Dec. 20, 1892). Thus she stressed the *uniqueness* of Jesus not just in terms of His sinlessness, but also in the blending of the human and divine.

The rest of this section (developments after 1888) will divide into two convenient parts, reviewing important expressions of (1) *uniqueness* and (2) *identity*. Once again, however, I must emphasize that you will find no startling or pathbreaking developments. But the intense nature of the debate over the relationship of the nature of Christ to the understanding of salvation demands a review of the most important statements that she made. We will first turn our attention to developments in her expressions of *uniqueness*.

Christ's Unique Humanity: 1889-1895

The first significant expression of *uniqueness* occurs in manuscript 16, 1890: "He stood before the world, from His first entrance into it, untainted by corruption, though surrounded by it" (7BC 907). In this instance she clearly spoke of Christ being untainted by corruption from His first entrance into the world. The statement presents the interesting implication that His lack of corruption had to do with His human, sinless inheritance, not just His character development on the earth.

This emphasis on the sinlessness of His inherited nature stands out clearly when compared with an earlier statement (1889) that referred to human corruption: "God will be better glorified if we confess the secret, *inbred* corruption of the heart to Jesus alone" (5T 645; italics supplied). Sinful humans have "inbred corruption," but Jesus was "untainted by corruption."

Of the terms Ellen White used to describe Christ's humanity, she never applied "corruption," "vile," "depravity," or "pollution" to the Saviour! In fact, she plainly declared that He was neither corrupt nor polluted.

One of her most striking expressions of *uniqueness* appears in manuscript 57, 1890. It is such an important statement that we will cite from it extensively. The general theme is that because of Christ's humanity, He was truly tempted.

"He had not taken on Him even the nature of angels, but humanity, *perfectly identical with our own nature, except without the taint of sin*. . . .

"But here we must not become in our ideas common and earthly, and in our perverted ideas *we must not think that* the liability of Christ to yield to Satan's temptations degraded His humanity and *He possessed the same sinful, corrupt propensities as man.*

"The divine nature, combined with the human, made Him capable of yielding to Satan's temptations. Here the test to Christ was far greater than that of Adam and Eve, for *Christ took our nature, fallen but not corrupted,* and would not be corrupted unless He received the words of Satan in the place of the words of God. . . .

"He descended in His humiliation to be tempted as man would be tempted, and His nature was that of man, capable of yielding to temptation. His very purity and holiness were assailed by a fallen foe, the very one that became corrupted and then was ejected from heaven. How deeply and keenly must Christ have felt this humiliation.

"How do fallen angels look upon this pure and uncontaminated One, the Prince of life . . ." (italics supplied).

Please note that she explicitly says that Christ took humanity, clearly identical to our own, except without the taint of sin. She further enforces this concept by warning that despite His liability to sin, we must not say that Jesus "possessed the same sinful, corrupt propensities as man." She then accentuates her point by declaring that "Christ took our nature, fallen but not corrupted, and would not be corrupted unless He received the words of Satan in the place of the words of God." Once more I invite the reader to carefully note what Ellen White says: "our nature," which is "fallen but not corrupted," is the nature that "Christ took" at the time of His incarnation, not what He achieved in His character development.

The concepts of manuscript 57, 1890, are some of the most forceful expressions of Christ's *uniqueness* that Ellen White ever made. In fact, their clarity has led Adventist scholar and editor Tim Crosby to suggest that this manuscript is almost as important as the famed Baker letter in our efforts to illuminate the nature of Christ's humanity.* It is at least an anticipation of what was to come in the Baker letter and a striking confirmation of her pre-1888 statements.

Her next significant statement occurs in manuscript 6, 1892, which utilized a thought that she would more forcefully express later on, especially in manuscript 50, 1900: "If we do our best . . . the humblest service may become a consecrated gift, made acceptable by the fragrance of His [Christ's] own merit" (PC 141). The thought here is that all that sinful humans do, even "our best," needs to be "made acceptable by the fragrance" of Christ's "own merit." Christ in His sinless humanity, combined with deity, has merit that sinful, even believing, humans don't have. Please note that while the justificationist usage of Christ's sinlessness is not surprising in this era, the concept of His sinlessness is nothing new at all.

Christ's Identity With Humanity: 1889-1895

Some important and clear expressions of His *identity* appear in Ellen White's writing during this period. She continued to use freely the expression "infirmities" during this entire era, but she strengthened it by declaring that "Jesus can be touched with the feeling of our infirmities" (RH, Oct. 1, 1889).

Christ's Example Portrayed in Our Nature

One of her most important expressions of *identity* showed up in numerous spirited responses to the declaration "that Christ could not have had the same nature as man, for if He had, He would have fallen under similar temptations" (see RH, Feb. 18, 1890). In a strong denial of such a concept, she repeatedly stated that it was necessary for Christ to "have man's nature" or "He could not be our example. If He was not a partaker of our nature, He could not have been tempted as man has been. If it were not possible for Him to yield to temptation, He could not be our helper." She then went on to make the usual sanctification application: "His temptation and victory tell us that humanity must copy the Pattern" (*ibid.*; 1SM 408).

She forcefully continued this line of thought in her more extended comments of 1892:

"But many say that Jesus was not like us, that He was not as we are in the world, that He was divine, and that we cannot overcome as He overcame." Her response was to quote Hebrews 2:16, 17: "Wherefore in all things it behoved him to be made like unto his brethren" (RH, Apr. 1, 1892).

In manuscript 1, written on November 13, 1892 (3SM 136-141), she replied to Satan's claim "that no man could keep the law of God after the disobedience of Adam." She did so by contending that Christ "passed over the ground where Adam fell, and endured the temptation in the wilderness, which was a hundredfold stronger than was or ever will be brought to bear upon the human race." Ellen White then said that Christ's overcoming "the temptations of Satan as a man" testified "to all the unfallen worlds and to fallen humanity that man could keep the commandments of God through the divine power granted to him of heaven."

Christ was "not only . . . a sacrifice for sin but" He came "to be an example to man in all things, a holy, human character." She forcefully highlighted the theme by the straightforward declaration that "the obedience of Christ by itself" was not "something for which He was particularly adapted, by His particular divine nature."

"If Christ had a special power which it is not the privilege of man to have, Satan would have made capital of this matter. . . .

"Bear in mind that Christ's overcoming and obedience is that of a true human being. . . . When we give to His human nature a power that it is not possible for man to have in his conflicts with Satan, we destroy the completeness of His humanity."

It is very clear in Ellen White's thought that Christ had no advantages in "His human nature," and this *identity* exalted "the completeness of His humanity."

This powerful *identity* statement concluded with these words:

"He came not to our world to give the obedience of a lesser God to a greater, but as a man to obey God's Holy Law, and in this way He is our example. . . .

"The Lord Jesus came to our world, not to reveal what a God could do, but what a man could do, through faith in God's power to help in every emergency. . . .

"Jesus, the world's Redeemer, could only keep the commandments of God in the same way that humanity can keep them."

Clearly Ellen White viewed Christ as giving the obedience of a man, which made Him the example for "what a man could do, through faith in God's power." Thus Jesus, as an example, keeps "the commandments of God in the same way that humanity can keep them."

The life of Christ was clear evidence that obedience is possible, as He was not "particularly adapted" either by "His particular divine nature" or a uniquely empowered human nature in obeying the will of God.

It should be apparent to us that whatever she understood the *uniqueness* of Christ's sinless human nature to be, it gave Him no particular advantage in dealing with temptation. His *identity* with humanity is complete enough to forestall any accusation of unfair advantage.

Once more, especially with these powerful declarations of Christ's *identity* in mind, we need to clearly define important terms. This will be the initial burden of the next chapter.

---

* This is a suggestion shared with the author in correspondence regarding the issue of Christ's humanity.

CHAPTER SIX

The Humanity of Christ and Salvation After 1888: Part II: Important Terms Defined

Christ's Nature Called "Fallen"

As in the pre-1888 era, Ellen White continued to use the word "fallen" as a description of Christ's "condition." It was qualified, however, with the expression of *uniqueness* that though He took "the nature of man in His fallen condition, . . . He did not take the taint of sin" (MS 93, 1893).[1] Thus "fallen" here does not have to do with "the taint of sin."

The Words "Passion," "Propensity," "Tendency," and "Inclination"

She continued to employ the word "passion" to express Christ's *identity*: "He had all the strength of the passion of humanity" (ST, Nov. 21, 1892).

What we have here is a morally nonqualified use of "passion." What do I mean by this? Such terminology is extremely critical to our understanding of Ellen White's Christology, and I urge the reader to follow patiently the analysis in the following paragraphs.

In previous presentations she had used expressions that went like this: Christ did not possess "the passions of our human, fallen natures" (2T 509, written in 1870), and though He is "a brother in our infirmities," He did *not* possess "like passions" (2T 202, written in 1869). Such expressions were *morally qualified*, and she clearly *contrasted* Christ's passion with what she called "the passions of our fallen natures" and distinguished them from our "like passions." She went on in *Testimonies for the*

Church, volume 2, page 202, to emphasize His *uniqueness* by *morally qualifying* His nature: she declared Him to be the "sinless One," and said that "His nature recoiled from evil."

Thus it is clear from previous usage that the phrase "all the strength of the passion of humanity" employed in the *Signs* of November 21, 1892, probably *referred to normal human desires, appetites, feelings, or emotions rather than perverted desires that naturally tend to break over the bounds of lawful expression.*

It seems wise to pause at this point to further clarify the meaning of the expressions "passion" and "propensities."

Larson has offered some helpful comments on the words "passion," "propensities," and "susceptibilities." After citing numerous usages in Ellen White's writings (Larson 22-25), he offers the following perceptive conclusions:

"In one usage, both words, *passions* and *propensities*, are used to describe something that Christians must control, but that by the very nature of things, they must retain and cannot eliminate from their experience. In this usage she tends to link the word *propensity* with such descriptive terms as *animal, human, natural*, etc. . . .

"In other usage, both words, *passions* and *propensities*, are used to describe something that Christians need not retain but must *eliminate*. Here control is not an adequate solution to the problem. In this usage she tends to link the word *propensity* with such descriptive terms as *evil, sinful, lustful*, etc. . . .

"In her references to Christ, she indicates that He had one class of passions and propensities, but did not have the other" (26).

Larson then illustrates his final point by comparing the two different Ellen White usages of "passion." He contrasts the statement "though He had all the strength of passion of humanity, never did He yield to temptation to do one single act which was not pure and elevating and noble" (undated MS 73; cf. IHP 155) with the declaration that "He was a mighty petitioner, not possessing the passions of our human fallen nature, but compassed with infirmities, tempted in all points like as we are" (2T 509).

It is quite evident that such expressions as "propensity," "passion," and "susceptibility," along with the little-used words "tendency"[2] and "inclination,"[3] all meant essentially the same thing, except when she qualified them with adjectives or adverbs freighted with moral distinctions. It seems clear that these expressions convey the idea that one has a proneness to do something, not an actual doing (either good or bad). Christ, however, did not possess a sinful proneness even though He had normal passions, tendencies, and propensities.

A Recent Study Helps to Clarify Terms

In the early 1980s an important study of Ellen White's use of literary sources shed some light on the meaning of the expressions "propensities" and "infirmities."

Ronald Graybill, Warren Johns, and Tim Poirier have shown that Ellen White used the sermons of Anglican minister Henry Melvill (1798-1871) in writing on the nature of Christ. They were able to do this important study because the White Estate possesses Ellen White's personal marked copy of Melvill's published sermons (*Melvill's Sermons*, 3rd ed.).

These careful researchers have demonstrated some instructive parallels between White's and Melvill's use of terminology. It is clear that Ellen White drew upon one of Melvill's sermons entitled "The Humiliation of the Man Christ Jesus" while she prepared an article entitled "Christ Man's Example" (RH, July 5, 1887).[4]

Not surprisingly, this sermon discusses Christ's humanity. Eric Webster gives us a helpful summation of Melvill's usage. "For Melvill there are two primary consequences of the fall: (1) 'innocent infirmities,' and (2) 'sinful propensities.' 'From both was Adam's humanity free before, and with both was it endowed after, transgression' (Melvill 47). By 'innocent infirmities' Melvill understands such characteristics as hunger, pain, weakness, sorrow and death. 'There are consequences on guilt which are perfectly guiltless. Sin introduced pain, but pain itself is not sin' (*ibid.*). By 'sinful propensities' Melvill refers to the proneness or tendency to sin.

"In his summary of the discussion, Melvill makes it clear that, in his view, Adam had neither 'innocent infirmities' nor 'sinful propensities;' we are born with both, and Christ took the first but not the second' (127, 128). Melvill plainly says that Christ had a humanity that was 'not prone to offend' (cited in Webster 128)."

Tim Poirier has "suggested that while Ellen White did not quote the words [of Melvill] (such as 'innocent infirmities,' 'sinful propensities' and 'prone to offend') the sentiments of Melvill could very well reflect Ellen White's own conviction' (ibid.)" (see Poirier).

"It is suggested that the apparent conflict found in Ellen White's statements on the humanity of Christ can be resolved in the context of Melvill's discussion. Could it be that when Ellen White states that Christ took upon Himself man's 'fallen and sinful nature' she is thinking of those 'innocent infirmities' that brought Christ to man's level, and that when she speaks of the sinlessness of Christ's humanity she is thinking of the fact that Christ did not possess 'sinful propensities'?" (Webster 128, 129).

Summation of the 1889-1895 Period

While the theme of the fully human Christ as the helper of "fallen man" against temptation continued as the dominant emphasis of this era, it is quite significant that the theme of the fully human and fully divine Christ who made a sinless sacrifice to justify penitent sinners came into full focus.

Ellen White's pre-1888 balance between Christ's full humanity and full deity continued to unfold and develop. But the justification application of His sinless humanity became fully explicit alongside the already well-developed theme (from the previous era) of the fully human and sinless Christ who can assist believers in the battle against temptation.

This period saw no crucial advances either in the expression of Christ's human *identity* or His *uniqueness*. By 1895 we can clearly say that she would make no further developments in the way she expressed Christ's *identity*. There would be further clarification during the next seven years, but only the *uniqueness* of Christ received additional illumination.

---

[1] Though Larson lists this statement as found in an undated MS 73, it was taken from Letter 27, May 29, 1892.

The verbatim published version appears in *The Signs of the Times*, Nov. 21, 1892.

[2] She never applies the expression "tendency to sin" to Christ, but often to other humans.

[3] Ellen White applied this expression to Christ at least three times. In the first two instances she clearly declared that He had no "inclination to corruption" (letter 8, 1895, to W.L.H. Baker) and that "His inclination to right was a constant gratification to His parents" (YI, Sept. 8, 1898). I address the third usage of the expression here only because Robert Wieland has chosen to interject it into the discussion of the Christological meaning of "inclination" ("The Golden Chain" 68).

First of all the reference: "Christ was put to the closest test, requiring the strength of all His faculties to resist the inclination when in danger, to use His power to deliver Himself from peril, and triumph over the power of the prince of darkness" (originally published in RH, Apr. 1, 1875; and cited in 7BC 930).

Wieland seems to imply that inclination, as used in this statement, means that Christ was tempted through such an "inclination" to commit an act of actual sin. If this is all that Wieland is implying, he is correct. But we must point out that here Ellen White is using "inclination" only in the sense that Christ had the natural human tendency (not "evil," "sinful," or "lustful") to use the advantage of His inherent divine power. This, however, is a far cry from the corrupt tendencies, propensities, and inclinations that all the rest of humanity are born with. Thus it is clear that she (in this instance) employs "tendency" only in a morally neutral way. In the first two instances cited above, however, she applied the term in clearly morally qualified senses: the first statement refers to an "inclination to corruption" (clearly sinful and never used to describe Christ), and the second statement speaks of "His inclination to right" (clearly something unique to Christ and morally positive and good).

[4] The results of this study appear in a 98-page document entitled *Henry Melvill and Ellen G. White: A Study of Literary and Theological Relationships* (Washington, D.C.: Ellen G. White Estate, 1982).

CHAPTER SEVEN

The Humanity of Christ and Salvation After 1888: Part 3: Developments From 1896 to 1902

Ellen White made some elaboration and clarification of Christ's humanity between 1896 and 1902. But it was His *uniqueness* that received most of her attention and special clarification, especially in the now-famous Baker letter written in late 1895 or early 1896. This letter has had such an important influence on the discussions about the meaning of Ellen White's Christology that I have placed a rather full discussion of it in the next chapter. She did, however, make other notable statements on the humanity of Christ during this period.

As in the two previous chapters, we will again use the general headings of *identity* and *uniqueness*. Let's first turn our attention to the statements about Christ's *identity*.

Christ's Identity With Humanity: 1896-1902

The Desire of Ages and Christology—When it comes to Ellen White's expression of Christ's profound unity or *identity* with human nature, we find few new developments during this important period of her writing career.

This fact might seem strange, even a bit shocking, when one considers that it was during these years that she completed her "Life of Christ" project with the publication of such books as *Thoughts From the Mount of Blessing* (1896), *The Desire of Ages* (1898), and *Christ's Object Lessons* (1900).

While *The Desire of Ages* is her most comprehensive work on the person of Christ and contains important statements about His humanity, it is crucial to realize that most of her statements about Christ's humanity in this much-revered work did not first appear in *The Desire of Ages*.

The simple fact is that in this work she mainly drew on her previous writings to express concepts that present Christ as profoundly *identified* with our humanity.

Though we have already mentioned it, it bears repeating that her most important gleaning from past publications was the obvious usage of the important and foundational article published in the *Review* of July 28, 1874. There she spoke of Christ taking "man's nature" after "the race had been weakened by four thousand years of sin" (DA 49), "decreasing in physical strength, in mental power, and in moral worth" (*ibid.* 117).

I do not in any way want to diminish the importance of the book *The Desire of Ages*. It is certainly the apex of her spiritual writing and is probably her most revered work. But for our purposes, it really contributes nothing original to the way she explains Christ's nature and the role that His humanity plays in our redemption.

Other Expressions of Identity—Ellen White also employed the rather sobering expression "sinful nature" to describe Christ's humanity (RH, Dec. 15, 1896). She used the term sparingly, with the *Review* statement of December 15, 1896, being republished several times (RH, Aug. 22, 1907; ST, July 30, 1902). Then she used it in a letter in 1902: "He took upon His sinless nature our sinful nature, that He might know how to succor those that are tempted" (letter 67, 1902; found in MM 181).

Although this expression "sinful nature" seems a bit shocking when applied to Christ's humanity, it seems clear that she meant it to convey the same idea as "fallen nature," "weakness," "degeneracy," and "infirmities." When this use of the term "sinful nature" is applied to Christ in this statement and compared with her use of a similar expression, "sinful, fallen condition" (a condition that would make Christ's atoning sacrifice unacceptable), it immediately becomes apparent that Ellen White can employ the expression "sinful nature" or "condition" in different ways. If a "sinful condition" can make His sacrifice ineffectual, it is obvious that this is an aspect of human nature that is considerably more viral and sinister than the meaning she gives to the expression "sinful nature" used in the present statement under consideration. In other words, it is one thing to be "affected by sin" and have a "sinful nature" but quite another matter to be "infected with sin" and have such an infection nullify the effectual nature of His sacrifice. If we do not see this distinction, we have put Ellen White in a gross contradiction.

Manuscript 166, dated December 15, 1898, deserves further attention because of its contribution to her expression of Christ's *identity*: "Christ did in reality unite *the offending nature* of man with His own sinless nature, because by this act of condescension, He would be enabled to pour out His blood in behalf of the fallen race" (later published in RH, July 17, 1900; italics supplied).

This somewhat unusual expression, "offending nature of man," seems, in context, to be equivalent to "the fallen race." By "offending nature" she could not possibly have in mind a nature that was actively sinning, as (whatever it meant) it was united to "His own sinless nature." It could refer to a nature that had the possibility of committing "offenses." What its precise meaning was is less clear than what it didn't indicate.

Christ's Unique Humanity: 1896-1902

While the book *The Desire of Ages* strongly emphasized Christ's *identity*, it did present some expressions of *uniqueness*. "Jesus Himself was free from physical deformity. . . . His physical structure was not marred by any defect; His body was strong and healthy" (50). In manuscript 18, 1898, she declared that "He was pure and uncontaminated by any disease."

In the thought of Ellen White, Christ was a first-century Jew, but despite His "weakness" and "infirmity," He had no physical defects. This is not true of all other human beings.

"He was a child . . . and spoke as a child; but no trace of sin marred the image of God within Him. . . . It was necessary for Him to be constantly on guard in order to preserve His purity" (DA 71).[1] The expressions "no trace of sin marred the image of God within Him" and that "His purity" was preserved imply a different nature than humans naturally possess.

Other Important Statements of Uniqueness—This period contributed six other notable affirmations of Christ's *uniqueness*:

1. "It is not correct to say, as many writers have said, that Christ was like all children. He was not like all children" (YI, Sept. 8, 1898). She then declared later in the same paragraph: "*His inclination to right* was a constant gratification to His parents" (*ibid.*; italics supplied). The next paragraph continued in the same vein. "No one, looking upon the child-like countenance, shining with animation, could say that Christ was just like other children" (*ibid.*).

I find this statement to be one of Ellen White's most forceful and un-equivocal declarations of Christ's *uniquely* sinless, human nature. The phrase "His inclination to right" is very compelling! Do you know any other human being who came into the world with an "inclination to right"?

2. "He was born without a taint of sin, but came into the world in like manner as the human family" (7BC 925). Here Ellen White was very clear that "without a taint of sin" referred to what He was born with—an obvious reference to His sinless nature. It does not seem to have primary reference to His history of flawless performance.

3. "Christ did in reality unite the offending nature of man with His own sinless nature, because by this act of condescension, He would be enabled to pour out His blood in behalf of the fallen race" (MS 166, 1898; later published in RH, July 17, 1900). The reader should note that we have already examined this statement from the perspective of its con-tribution to our understanding of Christ's *identity*. But it also makes an interesting comment on His *uniqueness*. It is clear that she had the be-ginning of the Incarnation in focus, as she referred to the union of the "offending nature of man" with "His own sinless nature." So "sinless na-ture" definitely referred to His heritage, not character development.

That the expression "His own sinless nature" alludes to the sinless-ness of His human nature, not His divine nature, receives strong support from another statement published in the same year: "Christ is a perfect representation of God on the one hand, and a perfect specimen of sinless humanity on the other hand" (7BC 907).

4. The thought that the best that humans (including "true believ-

ers") can do must be made "acceptable to God" by Christ's "own merit, which has no taint of earthly corruption," found fully matured expression in manuscript 50, 1900 (1SM 340-344).[2]

Ellen White declared that "the religious services, the prayers, the praise, the penitent confession of sin ascend from true believers" to the heavenly sanctuary. But since they pass through "the corrupt channels of humanity, they are so defiled that unless purified by blood, they can never be of value with God." Jesus, however, as "the Intercessor, who is at God's right hand, presents and purifies all by His righteousness." She then made this important declaration: "All incense from earthly taber-nacles" needs to be cleansed with the "drops of the blood of Christ. He holds before the Father the censer of His own merits, in which there is no taint of earthly corruption."

As was pointed out in chapter 2, this thought was but a further ex-pression of the implications of the intercessory ministry of Christ in heaven. But what is particularly relevant to Christology was the con-tention that even the best that believing humans can produce is tainted by earthly corruption. This is in clear contrast to the merits of Christ, which had no taint of earthly corruption. Sinful, believing humans need intercession, but Christ's sinless humanity does not.

5. "He was to take His position at the head of humanity by taking the nature but not the sinfulness of man" (ST, May 29, 1901). Note that this nature without "the sinfulness of man" was what He *took* and not what He *developed*. In other words, the strong implication was that a nature with-out sinfulness was His inheritance, not His character improvement.

6. "In Him was no guile or sinfulness; He was ever pure and undefiled; yet He took upon Him our sinful nature" (ST, July 30, 1902). Ellen White had expressed the same thought in a letter about three months earlier: "He took upon His sinless nature our sinful nature" (letter 67, 1902). Again the thought was what Christ *took*, not what He formed in character.

These last two statements offer a fitting opportunity to bring this de-velopmental survey to a preliminary conclusion. Fitting in the sense that the balanced, conversational tension of sinlessness and sinfulness was most simply expressed in these 1902 expressions. She declared the

Redeemer to be both "sinless" and "sinful" in nature, a delicate redemptive balance that she had made evident since 1868.

The 1896-1902 Period Summation

As in the previous period, this one also demonstrated very little new expression of Christ's *identity* with "fallen humanity."

It was in the area of expressing *uniqueness* that Ellen White's thought reached full maturity. This maturity, however, manifested itself in further clarification of expression rather than in stating entirely new concepts.

Certainly the year 1898 is the key year of full maturity in Ellen White's thinking on the humanity of Christ. To the already mature expressions of *identity* (which had arrived by 1893) came further clarifications of His *uniqueness* as the one without "evil propensities" and "inclinations" to corruption, born "without a taint of sin" in a "sinless nature."

Reflections on the 1889-1902 Era

First of all, we must again emphasize that the Christology of Ellen White reached its fully mature expression by the year 1888. About the only important development that took place afterward had to do with the concept of the blending of full, sinless humanity with complete deity (as necessary to an effectual, atoning sacrifice). This concept only came to a complete expression around 1890. While it had been foreshadowed in the earlier era, it does seem significant that its clearest statement came during the period of Ellen White's greatest emphasis on justification by faith in the death of Christ, our substitute.

Second, we must point out that after 1893 she made no further significant developments in her expression of *identity*.

The expressions of *uniqueness* did find further elaboration, but no really marked development came during this entire era.

One of the important questions that we need to ask at this juncture is why the important book *The Desire of Ages* mainly emphasized His *identity*. As was noted previously in this chapter, *uniqueness* was there, but the overwhelming expression was Christ's likeness to fallen humanity so that He could succor[3] in temptation. At the same time her other writings (letters, unpublished manuscripts, and periodical articles) continued to clearly express the *uniqueness* of His humanity. How are we to interpret this situation?

What appears to be going on is that, aside from the emphasis on the blending of His deity and humanity, there is simply no marked cause/effect relationship between her Christological expressions after 1888 and the remarkable developments that took place in her teachings on salvation. It is quite apparent that the Christological foundations of her thought had been clearly laid before 1888.

At the time (between 1888 and 1892) when she was giving her greatest accent to forgiveness and justification by faith in the merits of Jesus, she continued to emphasize Christ's *identity* with sinful humanity. And during the period when her published works gave great accent to the importance of sanctification and character perfection (1896-1902), she presented some of her most forceful expressions of the sinless *uniqueness* of Christ's humanity.

On balance, there seems to be no consistent evidence to demonstrate any sort of relationship between developments in Christology and salvation after 1888.

Ellen White's Unique Use of Christology

It might be of some interest to the reader to know that the forceful way Ellen White employed the humanity of Christ to express His role as one who can succor in temptation was unique in the American nineteenth-century religious revival of "holiness." No other individual promoting sanctification and the life of victory over sin appropriated the humanity of Christ as Ellen White did.

Such usage of the humanity of Christ found its most controversial expression, however, in her now-famous letter to W.L.H. Baker written in early 1896. The historical importance of this letter provides a most fitting juncture at which we can complete our historical survey in the next chapter.

---

[1] The theme of Christ's pure and sinless childhood found expression as early as the *Signs* of April 5, 1883: "The unsullied purity of the childhood, youth, and manhood of Christ, which Satan could not taint, annoyed him exceedingly." But it received its most forceful expression in the *Youth's Instructor*, Sept. 8, 1898.

[2] Once again we have come face-to-face with this important statement introduced in the final paragraphs of chapter 2 (which dealt with Ellen White's definition of sin). This statement contains a theme that had been developing since the 1870s, but that had become more explicit in the 1889-1892 period.

[3] This word is an old expression that simply means to give aid or help.

CHAPTER EIGHT

The Baker Letter

The Controversial Background

The so-called Baker letter was a rather lengthy epistle Ellen White sent to a certain W.L.H. Baker. Baker had had an extensive editorial career, but at the time he received his letter in early 1896[1] he was doing pastoral-evangelistic work on the island of Tasmania. The importance of the letter certainly doesn't derive from Baker's prominence in Adventist ministerial or editorial activities or the length of the document. Its basic significance arises out of five paragraphs discussing the humanity of Christ. Some further background on this letter's place in the history of Adventist discussions about Christology might prove helpful.

The discovery and initial publication of this letter in the mid-1950s was a wake-up call to the discussion of Christology. As already pointed out in chapter 1, until its publication there really had not been a significant pre-Fall versus post-Fall debate in Adventism. Its discovery was the main cause for the appearance of the pre-Fall school of thought and provoked a rather marked raising of consciousness about the many statements of Ellen White emphasizing Christ's sinless *uniqueness*. The lively, often contentious debate the letter sparked has yet to be fully resolved. Both the pre-Fall and post-Fall camps have made strenuous efforts to explain the document.

The arguments of both groups have been somewhat heated and forced, but it appears that the letter definitely has tilted the consensus of Adventist thinking in the direction of those who would emphasize the sinless *uniqueness* of Christ's humanity.

While the Baker letter has made a most important contribution to this debate, it is by no means absolutely essential to the establishment of Ellen White's position. Evidence already presented in previous chapters should make it clear that both camps in the debate have probably erred by not paying enough attention to the profoundly balanced tensions between the elements of "sinfulness" and "sinlessness" in Ellen White's thought.

Once again I invite the reader's closest attention to the following analysis and interpretation of the Baker letter. If for no other reason than its importance in sparking the present debate about Ellen White's understanding of Christology, this letter demands our careful examination. I also think the reader will be doctrinally and devotionally blessed by the carefully worded counsels of Ellen White on this critical subject.

The Context

As already mentioned, at the time he received his letter from Ellen White, Baker was pastoring and doing evangelism in Tasmania. Previous to this he had spent a number of years working at the Pacific Press in California and then had joined the newly founded Echo Publishing House in Australia. He had apparently found the transition from the more scholarly task of editing to pastoral-evangelistic ministry quite difficult. It was in these circumstances that Ellen White wrote him a lengthy letter of encouragement and counsel (Larson 310, 311).

It is readily apparent from the five critical paragraphs on the nature of Christ that Baker's thinking was not balanced. Apparently he was teaching that Christ had "inclinations to corruption."

Lyell V. Heise has argued that Baker most likely received his views (especially the concept that Christ had "inclinations to corruption") from prominent, contemporary Seventh-day Adventist writers (Heise 8-20). Such men clearly denied that Christ sinned by act, but they did proclaim the "mystery" that He had a "flesh laden with sin and with *all the tendencies to sin, such as ours is*" (italics supplied). This last quotation features the words of prominent Seventh-day Adventist editor and revivalist A. T. Jones (BE, Nov. 30, 1896).

Heise has also suggested that Ellen White was rebuking Baker for a

Christology that reflected the views of prominent Seventh-day Adventist preachers such as E. J. Waggoner and W. W. Prescott (Heise 16, 19, 20). A. Leroy Moore opposed Heise's suggestion with the contention that it "would . . . have been totally out of character for White to rebuke an obscure . . . young minister . . . to correct the errors of . . . prominent denominational theologians" (Moore 263).

The evidence is not really compelling on these issues one way or the other. I would suggest that what is clear is that Baker's understanding of the humanity of Christ was very similar to that of A. T. Jones, E. J. Waggoner, and W. W. Prescott. As to whether Ellen White would seek to rebuke them by writing a letter to the obscure Baker is really questionable. Ellen White seldom ever theologically corrected any prominent ministers. Often she would affirm the basic thrust of a man's ministry and overlook error in his teachings.[2] About the only exception to this rule was when she perceived that individuals were teaching concepts threatening one of the planks in the platform of "present truth."[3]

What, then, can we say about issues of context? On balance, it is apparent that all efforts to clarify the context have done little to shed any conclusive light on the meaning of the letter itself. It therefore seems that the document's Christology must stand on its own merits, and its doctrinal counsel is sufficiently clear in the immediate literary context.

The Letter's Major Burden

What is doctrinally clear is that the burden of the Baker letter had to do with distorted views of Christ's *humanity, not His deity*. Webster is quite correct when he argues that "a careful analysis of the context of the five paragraphs reveals clearly that the burden of Ellen White's thought is the humanity of Christ and not His divine nature" (130).

Analysis and Interpretation

I note some of the partisan arguments that this letter has inspired, but I would also remind the reader that our main effort here is to grasp what the letter contributes to a fuller understanding of Ellen White's Christology. While we simply cannot avoid such controversies, we will strive to be as objective as possible. It is quite probable that here, as in no other writing of Ellen White, we need to lay a contentious spirit aside and carefully search out the meaning of her words.

Interpretation of the Christological Paragraphs

As stated above, it is clear from the content of the letter that the major burden of the five key paragraphs on Christology was the humanity of Christ. After warning Baker to be "careful, exceedingly careful" in his teaching on the *"human nature* of Christ" (italics supplied), she warned him not to set Jesus "before the people as a man with the propensities of sin." This was in clear contrast to Adam's posterity, who were "born with inherent propensities of disobedience." Later in this same paragraph, after comparing Christ with the unfallen Adam, she reinforced her point with the phrase that "not for one moment was there in Him an evil propensity."

What Is an "Evil Propensity"?—One of the key issues in interpreting the letter is the meaning of the word "propensity."[4] The *identity* advocates have made strenuous efforts to make it appear that *"propensity* implies a 'response to gravity,' 'a definite hanging down,' instead of resistance. It definitely connotes actual participation in sin, and Ellen White used the word in its finest English connotation" (Wieland, *The 1888 Message* 62).

First of all, Wieland's suggested interpretation of "propensity" goes against the usual and common everyday sense in which people use the word. One is curious as to what dictionary or thesaurus Wieland consulted that enables him to justify his suggestion that the term "propensity" implies an "actual participation in sin."[5]

Wieland has proposed that "propensities of sin," an "evil propensity," or "inclination to corruption" only imply that Christ actually "yielded to corruption." He denies that such expressions refer to proclivities, or a proneness, to sin.

In other words, by equating "propensity to sin" with actual acts of yielding to sin, Wieland takes away the clear intent of Ellen White's message, which goes something like the following: When she says Christ had no propensity or proclivity to sin, she only meant that He did not participate in actual acts of sin. Thus Christ, according to Wieland, did have, just like sinful humans, proclivities to sin—He simply did not yield to them.

It seems clear to this writer that Ellen White was saying to Baker that Christ had neither sinful propensities in His human nature nor actual acts of sin in His life record.

Second, Wieland ignores the way Ellen White used "propensity" in the immediate literary context of the letter. She spoke of Adam's posterity being "born with inherent propensities of disobedience." Eric C. Webster has persuasively maintained that "if one is born with such a propensity one would question Wieland's definition of 'propensity'" as "'actual participation in sin'" (Webster 132).

Certainly Ellen White's own usage of the term should determine its meaning in this context. It seems clear that "propensities of sin," "inherent propensities of disobedience," and "an evil propensity" are all expressions describing what Adam's children are born with, not their character development. The obvious implication, however, is that Christ was not born with such natural inclinations to sin.

The Adam/Christ Comparison Continued—She declared that "Adam was created a pure, sinless being, without a taint of sin upon him." Then two paragraphs later she plainly admonished Baker to "never, in any way, leave the slightest impression upon human minds that a taint of or inclination to corruption rested upon Christ."

Again, the context of the Christ/Adam comparison strongly suggests that her expression that Christ was "without a taint of sin" refers to His natural inheritance as *comparable* to (not *contrasted* with) the "pure, sinless" "first Adam," whom God "created . . . without a taint of sin upon him." Thus it seems fair to conclude that the phrase no "taint of or inclination to corruption" refers to the human nature that Christ naturally came into the world with—in clear contrast to what corrupt humans are born with.

Also, the close association of the expressions "inclination to corruption" (which Christ did not have) and "a taint of . . . corruption" (which Christ also did not have) strongly suggests that the two expressions were *equivalent* in meaning.

Furthermore, it seems most obvious that the meaning of the word "inclination" is here equivalent to "propensity." As noted earlier in this chapter (especially footnote 5), a quick glance at any dictionary or thesaurus of the English language (either contemporary to Ellen White or from our time) clearly demonstrates that "propensity" is equated with "tendency." Furthermore, not one of the dictionary entries comes close to suggesting that the terms "propensity" and "inclination" (or any of their synonyms) imply an "actual participation in sin." Thus it is quite evident that these expressions referred to natural tendencies, leanings, or a bent toward sin. Christ did not possess them, and this was clearly in *contrast* to Adam's posterity, who did!

An Important Consideration—The key sentence referred to in the previous two paragraphs needs some further analysis. She plainly admonished Baker: "Never, in any way, leave the slightest impression upon human minds that a taint of or inclination to corruption rested upon Christ, or that He in any way yielded to corruption."

Her obvious intent was to warn Baker to present Christ as one who was sinless both in nature (in the sense that no "taint of or inclination to corruption rested upon Christ") and actions (He never "in any way yielded to corruption"). She *did not equate* the expression "a taint of or inclination to corruption" with the expression "yielded to corruption." This point rejects Wieland's interpretation.

Wieland contends that "Ellen White equated the idea of 'a taint of, or inclination to, corruption' *resting* on Christ as the same as His *yielding* to 'corruption'" (Wieland, *An Introduction* 33).[6] In other words, he sees "a taint of or inclination to corruption" as being explained or defined by the expression "He . . . never . . . in any way yielded to corruption."

It is apparent that Wieland's interpretation has distorted her meaning in this sentence. Ellen White obviously meant to express the thought that Christ was sinless in the sense that He had *neither* an "inclination to corruption" *nor* a personal history in which He actually "yielded to corruption." "Inclination to" and "yield[ing] to" are two closely related but definitely distinguishable concepts. I respectfully submit that Wieland's theological agenda has forced an *equation* of meanings in which a *distinction* is clearly the intentional message Ellen White sought to convey.

Uniqueness Further Clarified—The Baker letter has some further expressions of *uniqueness*. She referred to Christ as "that holy thing" and then proceeded to express the "mystery that is left unexplained that Christ could be tempted in all points like as we are, and yet be without sin."

Ellen White saw a "mystery" in the fact that Christ was "without sin" and that this sinlessness of Christ (in not yielding to temptation) is a part of the larger mystery of the "incarnation of Christ [that] has ever been, and will ever remain a mystery." She did not attempt to explain this mystery, but simply declared the unique fact that (for whatever reasons) Christ did not yield to sin.

It is interesting that she then advised Baker to "let every human being be warned from the ground of making Christ altogether human, such an one as ourselves; for it cannot be."

As stated earlier, it is quite possible that Baker was presenting Christ as having both "inclinations to" and an actual "yielding to" corruption. Ellen White understood the mystery of His *uniqueness* as precluding both. Whatever his views were, it is clear that she opposed the views that Christ either sinned by actual acts of transgression (yielding to corruption) or had inclinations to corruption.

Summation

While the Baker letter has not decisively settled the debate about the nature of Christ, it has played an important role. It has certainly been a compelling statement in support of the so-called pre-Fall position, and the supporters of the post-Fall[7] teaching have struggled with it valiantly. But as the dust has begun to settle in this lengthy theological debate, it seems that the message of the Baker letter clearly weighs in on the "pre-Fall" side. Its terminology obviously seems to point to a profoundly sinless *uniqueness* in the nature of Christ.

It is tempting at this point to weigh in with my own personal understanding of Ellen White's overall view on Christology. I have certainly given some strong hints as to my own views of her teaching, but a fuller statement of my interpretation has to await the final section of this work. It is to this interpretive section that we now turn our attention.

---

[1] The Ellen G. White Estate has listed this document as letter 8, 1895, and it appears in volume 5 of *The Seventh-day Adventist Bible Commentary* (pp. 1128, 1129). Although it is dated 1895, Lyell Heise, in "The Christology of Ellen G. White Letter 8, 1895," has presented evidence that it was actually written in 1896.

[2] Probably the best examples of this were the numerous persons who held Arian positions on the nature of Christ, but received no rebuke for their Arian thinking (here Uriah Smith immediately comes to mind).

[3] Prime examples of such rebukes were her strong testimonies given to Dr. J. H. Kellogg and Albion F. Ballenger. Both men held views that she felt subtly undermined the Adventist position on the sanctuary doctrine.

[4] For a detailed discussion of Ellen White's use of the word "propensity," we urge the reader to review the discussion in chapter 6.

[5] Although Wieland does refer to the *Oxford English Dictionary* as defining the meaning of propensity to be "to hang or lean forward or downward," *nothing was discovered* in any of the standard dictionaries (including the *Oxford English Dictionary*) that comes even close to supporting Wieland's suggestion that "propensity" be understood to imply "a 'response to gravity,' 'a definite hanging down,' instead of resistance." Wieland then goes on to claim that propensity "definitely connotes actual participation in sin, and Ellen White used the word in its finest English connotation" (Wieland, *The 1888 Message*, p. 62). The following standard dictionaries fail to support Wieland's suggested definition of "propensity": *Funk and Wagnalls New Standard Dictionary of the English Language* (New York: Funk and Wagnalls, 1945); *Webster's New International Dictionary of the English Language*, second ed., unabridged (Springfield, Mass.: G. & C. Merriam Co., 1934); *Oxford Universal English Dictionary on Historical Principles* (New York: Oxford University Press, 1936, Vol VII); *A New English Dictionary on Historical Principles* (popularly known as *Oxford English Dictionary*) (Oxford: The Clarendon Press, 1909 Vol. VII); *The American Heritage Dictionary of the English Language* (New York: American Heritage Publishing Co., Inc., 1969); *Encyclopaedic Dictionary*, new revised (Boston: Newspaper Syndicate, 1897).

[6] Wieland seems to suggest the same interpretation of this portion of the Baker letter in "*The Golden Chain*," pp. 68, 69.

[7] I want the reader to understand that I use the expressions pre-Fall and post-Fall in this context as only a concession to the unhappy history that we are talking about. I have tried to use my suggested terms—*identity* and *uniqueness*—and will continue to do so except when I have to speak of history.

A Chronological Study

Section 4

INTERPRETATIONS AND IMPLICATIONS

CHAPTER NINE

Christ's Humanity, Justification, and Perfection

E llen White's view of Christ's humanity contains many elements of mystery. Furthermore, because we find statements that seem hard to reconcile with one another, some have even concluded that she was simply contradictory in her presentations on Christology. I would firmly suggest that such a charge not only is harsh but also represents a lack of appreciation for two key elements in her thought.

Central Factors in Ellen White's Understanding

The first element is the striking doctrinal consistency in a large body of writings produced over the course of six decades by a thinker who wasn't attempting to do an academic, systematic, or technically doctrinal work.

She did not confine her comments on the nature of Christ to any one major work, but scattered them throughout her writings. Often they showed up in rather surprising settings. My observation is very similar to Eric C. Webster's: "The general consistency in Ellen White's views over a considerable span of time is a testimony to her clarity of thought" (149).

The second factor is that her views are more than just noncontradictory; I would strongly suggest that these seemingly irregular features are what give her thought its power and depth. Ellen White could sound like the author of the book of Hebrews when she discussed Christ's profound *identity* with humanity and John the Beloved (John 8:46) when she discussed His amazing *uniqueness*.

Causes for Misunderstanding

The problems in understanding Ellen White have arisen when her interpreters have (1) wanted to emphasize one aspect of His humanity to the neglect of the other, or (2) when they have attempted to totally resolve a mystery that can't be solved by human minds. If there were no mystery, what need would there be for faith?

For Ellen White, the stress on *uniqueness* or *identity* seemed to depend largely on what doctrinal issue she was dealing with.

When she spoke of victory over sin and Christ's power to sustain struggling sinners, she was more likely to emphasize *identity*. But when she presented Christ as a sinless, sacrificial substitute and one who is able to free us from the guilt of sin, she would emphasize *uniqueness*.

Christ's Sinless Uniqueness and "Sinful Nature"

Though His "spiritual nature was free from every taint of sin" (ST, Dec. 9, 1897; 5BC 1104), He was a rather typical first-century human being. It seems best to express the freedom of His "spiritual nature" from sin this way: He was *affected* by sin but not *infected* with it.

Ellen White was clear that He took "our sinful nature" (7-ABC 453), but only in the sense of a *lessened capacity* as a result of the principle of physical inheritance.[1] He was weak, frail, infirm, degraded, degenerate, deteriorated, wretched, and defiled, but somehow He was *not* "altogether human, such an one as ourselves; for it cannot be" (5BC 1129).

Whatever this *lessened capacity* involved, it did *not* include (1) yielding to corruption (He never committed an act of sin) or (2) "a taint of sin" or "an evil propensity" in His sinless "spiritual nature" (ST, Dec. 9, 1897; 5BC 1128). While Christ *was not just like* fallen humans, He *was enough like* them to identify with their "infirmities" in their struggle with temptation. His nature, however, *was enough unlike* them to be a sinless, substitutionary sacrifice.

Some Compelling Implications About Sin

Such conclusions about Christ's sinlessly *unique* nature receive strong support from some powerful implications arising out of Ellen

White's understanding of sin and sinfulness. Let's refresh our thinking on the issues and questions in chapter 2.

First, could Jesus have had the very same nature that we receive from sinful Adam and still be our Saviour? Let's be even more explicit with Ellen White's terminology: Could Jesus be our saving, sacrificial substitute and still be called "naturally depraved" (IHP 163), "corrupt" (1SM 344), and be characterized as having "inherent propensities of disobedience" (5BC 1128), "hereditary and cultivated tendencies to evil" (CT 20), or "a bent to evil" (Ed 28, 29)? Could Jesus save babies born with the "inheritance" of "selfishness . . . inwrought in" their "very being" if He had been born with the same "inheritance" of "selfishness" (HS 138, 139)? I would like to confess that the answer to such compelling questions should be a firm no!

It is quite obvious that the thought of Ellen White contains an inherent demand that in some important respects Jesus had to be *uniquely* sinless. It had to be true not only of His acts but also of His inherited nature. The reason for this is that if He was sinful in either His acts or inherited nature, He could not be an effectual Saviour from sin. Such a conclusion becomes almost overwhelmingly compelling when we recall the following statement:

"Man could not atone for man. His sinful, fallen condition would constitute him an imperfect offering, an atoning sacrifice of less value than Adam before his fall."

Two paragraphs later she says:

"Christ alone could open the way, by making an offering equal to the demands of the divine law. He was perfect, and undefiled by sin. He was without spot or blemish" (RH, Dec. 17, 1872).

Second, I would suggest that Ellen White's understanding of Jesus' role as our constantly available intercessor calls for a powerful accenting of the sinless *uniqueness* of His human nature. Once again we need to remind ourselves about the pointedly practical applications of her view of Christ's intercession. Such application reached its climactic expression in manuscript 50, 1900 (found in 1SM 344): "Oh, that all may see that everything in obedience, in penitence, in praise and thanksgiving, must be placed upon the glowing fire of the righteousness of Christ." Again I would point out to the reader that in this important statement she was clearly referring to "the religious services, the prayers, the praise, the penitent confession of sin" that "ascend from *true believers* . . . to the heavenly sanctuary, but passing through *the corrupt channels of humanity*, they are so defiled that unless purified by blood, they can never be of value with God" (italics supplied).

I find the implications of this provocative statement quite powerful! Once again it seems more forceful to focus these implications with a question: Could Jesus have a *nature just like ours* and still be our interceding advocate and high priest? If we, with our defiled and corrupt channels of humanity, need the constant intercession of Jesus, *could Jesus intercede for us if His human nature was also defiled and corrupt?* Again the question demands a resounding no!

Furthermore, the most compelling implication for ignoring this aspect of Ellen White's thought is the way that the so-called "post-Fall" interpreters always seem to want to downgrade the importance of justification. We note a disturbing tendency to collapse justification into sanctification, making the fruits of sanctified obedience part of the meritorious ground or basis of our acceptance with God (see the exchange with Kevin Paulson in chapter 11).

The danger in such a tendency has always been to return believers to the severe spiritual bondage so poignantly typified in John Wesley's experience before he came to a clear understanding of the proper relationship between justification and sanctification. The change in his experience (knowing that justification was the ground of sanctification, not vice versa) did not lead him to indulge in an attitude of cheap grace; but it did give Wesley a firm "ground" of assurance to grow in obedience. Please note Ellen White's perceptive observation: "He continued his strict and self-denying life, not now as the *ground*, but the *result* of faith; not the *root*, but the *fruit* of holiness" (GC 256).

While believers are saved *experientially* by living faith (active trust) and *evidentially* (even conditionally) by sanctified works, we are saved *meritoriously* only by the merits of Christ's life and death, which are forensically or legally reckoned and accounted to us through His constant intercession in heaven.

Christian obedience, "through the righteousness of Christ . . . wrought by His Spirit working in and through us," might be the "ground of our hope" for deliverance from the power of sin (see *Steps to Christ*, p. 63), but it can never be the meritorious ground or basis of our acceptance with Christ—either before or after conversion. If such were the case, it would create enormous spiritual problems. Christians would tend to fall into one of the ditches on either side of the highway to heaven. Either they would be tempted to think too highly of themselves (the ditch of self-righteousness) or they would end up in the anxiety that results from constantly looking to self to see if their subjective performance is good enough to merit salvation (the ditch of dispair).[2]

For Ellen White, the keystone that keeps justification and sanctification in proper balance is the intercessory ministry of Christ, which constantly reckons trusting (not presumptuous) believers to be perfect through justification and also constantly empowers growth in grace through sanctification. But if Jesus is inherently sinful in nature, He cannot be our effectual, interceding advocate.

In addition to these compelling implications drawn from Ellen White's definition of sinful human nature and her clear testimony that Christ had no "taint of sin" or "evil propensity" in His sinless "spiritual nature" (ST, Dec. 9, 1897; 5BC 1128), we need to consider one more provocative line of evidence for His sinless *uniqueness*.

A Very Stubborn Fact

The arguments of those who claim that Christ had to be *just exactly like* sinful humans in order to identify with them break down over one stubborn fact of human history: We have all sinned, but Christ never did. Think about that for a moment.

A previous experience in sin always strengthens the force of temptation. The desire to commit any specific act of sin will be more powerful for the one who has already done it than it will be for someone who has never indulged in it. Does this make Christ unable to succor or identify with us in our temptations?

Eric Webster forcefully lays out the relentless logic of the situation: "Right here there remains a massive gap between Christ and the sinner. At best, Christ can only face initial temptation, but He cannot be brought down to the level of the alcoholic who faces the temptation to indulge in strong drink for the thousandth time. . . . Christ never knew the power of habitual sin and cannot meet fallen man on that level" (419). Any attempt to drag Him down fully to our level collapses "on the bedrock" of our history of universally "habitual sin" (ibid. 420).

Can Christ Really Identity With Us?

Let's face the practical issue squarely: If Christ's *identity* involves (1) no history of habitual sin and (2) not being born with tendencies and propensities to sin, how then can He really identify with us in our struggle with temptation? Can such a sinlessly *unique* Person really be of help to us who are born with such tragic histories and corrupt, depraved tendencies?

I would suggest that Christ did not need to be born with either a bent to sin or a history of sinning to feel the power of temptation. Upon further reflection, it becomes obvious that the basis of His temptations was not an inherently corrupt nature or sordid history of sin, but the possibility of using His full deity to resist the wiles of the devil.

In other words, the key temptation for Christ was the same as it is for all humans—the desire to go it alone and depend upon self rather than divine, imparted power from above. The history of Adam and Eve, along with one third of the heavenly angels, ought to give us a clue about a simple fact of human experience: *Having natural tendencies to sin is not essential to being tempted.* Certainly God did not create our first parents flawed in any way. Yet they yielded to temptation.

Morris Venden has illustrated the central dynamics involved in temptation: People who drive "wimpy" cars do not struggle with the urge to "stomp it." They know that they don't have it "under the hood." But the people who are most tempted to speed are the ones who have what we used to refer to as "440 under the hood"! Christ had infinite, divine power "under the hood," and His great temptation was to depend on self rather than the imparted power of the divine Father.

Let's Allow the Balance to Stand!

If we permit Ellen White's finely tuned balance to stand as it is, her doctrine of Christ's humanity has an appealing wholeness. When we lose sight of one side of the balance, or deny it, her thought becomes distorted and can easily be perverted into "believe, only believe" presumption or discouragingly self-centered, behavioristic extremes. Ellen White sought to uphold the delicate balance and constantly battled the extremes.

A Final Appeal

Once again I urgently suggest that we lay aside the more traditional expressions such as pre-Fall and post-Fall in this important search for doctrinal clarity! They are simply inadequate to express the richness of Ellen White's understanding of the humanity of Christ.

When it came to Christ as a fully sinless, sacrificial substitute, she was pre-Fall. But when she wrote of His ability to sustain in times of temptation, she emphasized His *identity* and spoke largely in post-Fall terms. A careful balancing of the terms *uniqueness* and *identity* seems to reflect more accurately the profoundly rich tensions involved in this heavy theme.

Such a balance certainly involves some aspects of mystery. In fact, I am suggesting the use of such technical words as "balanced tension," "dialectic," or "paradox" to express her profound balance between Christ's "sinful" and "sinless" nature. But such expressions of mystery and complexity are not unique to me.

I found it very interesting (and comforting) to discover that even writers who seem to argue for the strong *identity*, or the so-called post-Fall position, also want to speak in terms of some tentativeness that evidences a recognition of a mysteriously balanced tension. Gil G. Fernandez speaks of "ambiguities" (29) and A. Leroy Moore uses the expression "paradoxical dimensions" (249).[3]

Furthermore, it does not seem to be accidental that their expressions come close to those of Eric C. Webster (a forceful defender of the sinless *uniqueness* position—essentially what the pre-Fall people argue for,) who wants to use such terms as "dialectical" (99) and "paradox, tension and antithesis" (153).

It seems that a setting of some mystery and tension, with a balanced use of the terms *uniqueness* and *identity*, best expresses her meaning. This allows each concept to make its essential contribution to her very sensible and useful Christology.

As we bring this summation chapter to a close, it is important to remember an important fact: The main purpose of Ellen White's reflections and presentations on the humanity of Christ was to serve the needs of a very practical understanding of the experience of salvation. Unless Jesus is seen as profoundly and sinlessly *unique*, He really cannot justify us. And if He is not deeply *identified* with our weakness, He will be unable to truly succor or help us in our struggles with temptation. But in the profound and comprehensive view of Ellen White, He was sufficiently both to be our complete Redeemer!

---

[1] I must confess that I am indebted to Desmond Ford for the essential phrasing of this sentence.

[2] The great adversary is always attempting to entice believers to look to self (both our triumphs and failures) or the faults of others rather than to Christ (see *Steps to Christ*, p. 71). Ellen White is especially subtle in her analysis of this phenomenon when she lays down the following insight: "The CLOSER you come to Jesus, the more faulty you will appear in your own eyes; for your vision will be clearer, and your IMPERFECTIONS will be seen in distinct contrast with His perfect character. Be not discouraged; this is an evidence that Satan's delusions are losing their power" (BE, Dec. 1, 1892; cf. SC 28, 29, 64, 65). How can those who are coming closer to Jesus have any confidence in their acceptance with God unless they know that they are accepted through the objective, justifying merits of Jesus in His constant heavenly intercession? If they are dependent on the work that Jesus is doing through them to be the ground of their acceptance, they will never have gospel confidence, as they will always be growing in a clearer understanding of their defects.

Justification, which is grounded on the subjective work of Christ in the soul (the sanctifying grace of the Spirit), has evolved into a vicious cycle for all too many believers—especially those with very sensitive consciences. It is little wonder that so many such people have been driven either to dispair or subtle self-righteousness. Dispair is the major pitfall of the most sensitive in nature, while Pharisaic externalism and superficial behaviorism is the tragic lot of those lost in the mists of subtle self-righteousness (cf. Phil. 3:4-7).

[3] In his earlier work, *The Theology Crisis*, A. Leroy Moore seemed to be arguing for a post-Fall interpretation of Ellen White's writings. But after a closer reading of this work and his more recent *Adventism in Conflict*, it is clear that Moore's somewhat complex principles of doing theology led him to seek to balance what he felt was Desmond Ford's overemphasis on Christ's pre-Fall uniqueness. Moore's "paradoxical" principles (not being used in a polemical setting such as *The Theology Crisis*) have led him to come out forthrightly for what is essentially the pre-Fall position in his recently released *Adventism in Conflict*.

CHAPTER TEN

To "Historic Adventism": A Proposal for Dialogue and Reconciliation[1]

During the past few years individuals and groups that have reacted strongly to a range of questions facing the Seventh-day Adventist Church have used the expression "historic Adventism" to identify their particular understanding of these issues. The issues in question include the atonement, the humanity of Christ,[2] the emphasis on justification by faith, 1888 and its meaning, the Desmond Ford crisis (and other threats to the sanctuary doctrine), Walter Rea and challenges to the authority and integrity of Ellen White, styles of worship, and Adventist lifestyle concerns. They use "historic Adventism" to imply strongly that the "historical" interpretation is the "orthodox" and "traditional" brand of standard Adventism.[3]

The comments in this chapter dealing with historic Adventism's claims regarding Adventist doctrinal orthodoxy will largely be restricted to the nature of Christ, especially His humanity. But before we begin our examination of the relationship of the nature of Christ to the central truths that have historically defined Adventist theology, I would first of all like to confess my convictions regarding the absolute centrality of Christ.

Adventist theology has confessed Christ's full divinity (as the second person of the divine Trinity) and His full humanity. The issue that has divided the church, especially in the past 40 years, has to do with just how closely Christ "identified" with humanity.

The so-called historic Adventists have wanted to elevate their distinctive views on the humanity of Christ to the level of a "pillar" or plank in the "platform of present truth." Is there evidence from Ellen White and the Adventist history of doctrinal development to support such a claim?

Certainly confessing the full humanity of Christ has become a part of the Adventist doctrinal heritage and absolutely central to a full understanding of how God goes about redeeming the lost. But can we raise the particular understandings and teachings of the "historics" (or any Adventists) to the same status?

Clarification of Terminology

Instead of "historic" or "traditional Adventism," I would suggest the following: "Christian, or eternal, verities" for basic doctrines embraced by Adventists and held by most other Christians,[4] "essential Adventism" for that which is distinctively Adventist, "processive Adventism" for those issues that are important but still unsettled, and "nonessential Adventism"[5] to describe that which is interesting, but not central to Adventist self-understanding.

In view of the terms I have suggested as the framework for the discussion to follow, I would suggest that we see the confession of Christ's full deity and humanity as a part of the "Christian, or eternal, verities" that Adventism confesses with the larger Christian tradition. As to the issue of just how identical His full humanity is to our sinful nature, I would tentatively suggest that we place this question in the category of "processive Adventism" rather than "essential Adventism." Is there evidence from both Ellen White and Adventist history to support the classifications I have suggested? Before answering this question, let's take a closer look at the expression "historic Adventism."

Historic Adventism: The Perplexing History

In addition to the divisive and polemical connotations of such expressions as "historic Adventism," I would suggest some historical reasons for regarding the term as of questionable value in Adventist theological discussion and development.

One does not have to study very far into Adventist history before discovering numerous theological wrecks lying on the Adventist doctrinal highway. They certainly qualify as historic, but they have not stood the test of time and theological scrutiny.[6] The semi-Arianism of many of our most prominent pioneers is a theological dead letter today (Schwarz 167, 168, 395ff.).[7] I have not met an Adventist Arian in my lifetime! Yet Arianism is part of Adventist history and could qualify *historically* as historic Adventism! We could say the same of early views about when the Sabbath should begin, early understandings of Systematic Benevolence, the personhood of the Holy Spirit, and the shut door. Could it be that some views presently held as very near and dear to historic (and other) Adventists will go the way of Arianism?

We should also mention that such issues as the human nature of Christ, the interpretation of 1888, and the meaning of Christian perfection have always had differing interpretations in the Adventist doctrinal tradition. It is becoming clearer to this writer, a self-confessed former post-Fall perfectionist, that advancing research suggests that the so-called historic Adventists have no corner on any orthodox understanding of these issues.

Christ's Humanity: A Brief Interpretive History

While Ralph Larson has demonstrated (in *The Word Was Made Flesh*) that a rather strong consensus on a post-Fall view existed until the middle 1950s, George Knight has also shown that there was provocative opposition to the post-Fall view of none other than A. T. Jones in the mid-1890s (Knight 132-150).

I would also submit that the interpretation of 1888 that holds that the key emphases generated by that crisis were the post-Fall view of Christ's humanity and the issue of perfection is becoming more suspect with advancing research (Knight 36ff.). While it is true that Jones and Waggoner were strong proponents of the post-Fall view of Christ's humanity and perfection, one searches the 1888 comments of Ellen White in vain for any statements that emphasize the humanity of Christ and perfection as major Minneapolis issues.[8] To the contrary, it is becoming clearer that 1888 represented a theological crisis and was, in the thinking of Ellen White, *primarily* a crisis brought on by a misunderstanding of justification by faith and a lack of charity in theological discourse.[9]

"Essential Adventism" Further Clarified Historically

As mentioned above, I am proposing the expression "essential Adventism"[10] as a more inclusive, workable term in seeking to resolve what we mean by distinctive Adventism. I am suggesting that it would include doctrines and issues that have (1) achieved wide consensus and (2) given Adventism its distinctive theological and practical flavor, as opposed to what I have called "processive" issues.

Consider a few of the following historical precedents and some of the implications they suggest:

1. Adventism and Creeds—Adventism has always taken a rather dim view of creeds, and it seems as though the persons who use such expressions as historic Adventism would very much like to see Adventism go a strongly creedal route—the implication being that if you don't see it our way, you are not a sound Adventist and are opening up a Pandora's box of compromise, sin, and degenerate apostasy. Such attitudes do not seem to fit the mold of the anticreedal, broader Adventist theological framework.

2. The Tension Between the "Pillars" and "New Light"—A tension has always existed between the "pillars" of present truth and "new light." An essential conservatism in Adventist theological formation has always pulled back when new light has been proposed, but there has also been a clear understanding that "we have many lessons to learn, and many, many to unlearn" (CWE 37; also see Schwarz 393, 394).

So while we have things to conserve, we also have things to let go of and new things to pick up on. If we get too tight and too specific, we may frustrate the work of the Holy Spirit in bringing forth fresh insights from the Word of God.

Adventism's "Essential" Doctrinal Framework

What should be the Christian and "essential" framework of Adventist theological discourse?

First the broadly Christian. Adventism is primarily Christian in the sense of upholding the great verities of the faith. We strongly affirm such doctrines as the full deity of Christ, the Trinity, the personhood of the Holy Spirit, the bodily resurrection of Christ, and the Lord's Supper.

In a more focused way, we are thoroughly Protestant in that we take biblical authority as the court of last resort in matters of faith and practice (as opposed to tradition, ecclesiastical authority, and even postbiblical prophets or revelations) and emphasize justification by faith, not human works, as the basis of salvation.

I would further suggest that we have appropriated important strands from (1) Wesleyanism/Arminianism, especially in our form of church governance, God's respect for the integrity of human choice, and emphasis on the importance of sanctification; (2) Restorationism, with its emphasis on seeking to restore the primitive simplicity of the New Testament church, building "the old waste places," repairing "the breach," and restoring "paths to dwell in" (Isa. 58:12); and (3) the Baptist tradition, with its emphasis on believers' baptism by immersion and religious freedom.

We are thus broadly in agreement with the basic orthodoxy of the Christian tradition and we are thoroughly Protestant. All of this is certainly essential to our Christian self-understanding. Adventism, however, has a more distinctive, essential cast that goes beyond the great eternal verities of our Christian and Protestant heritages.

Before we venture a suggestion as to what the distinctive essentials of Adventism might be, we should first ask what constitutes the theological essentials of a given tradition. It seems that theological essentials consist of doctrines and practices that a tradition could not do without and still retain its unique identity. Such a tradition might share numerous theological commonalities with other traditions, but such distinctive essentials would be what give it its special identity.

Perhaps we can best illustrate this distinctiveness by a brief comparison of Adventism with Confessional Lutheranism.

Adventists want to affirm justification by faith and the "presence" of Jesus in the sacrament of the Lord's Supper. Adventism, however, has not been comfortable with the Confessional Lutheran emphasis on "faith alone" that has tended to exclude an emphasis on sanctification. Neither have we accepted the liturgical, literalistic understanding of "presence" in the Lord's Supper. As Adventists we have tended to see the elements as more symbolic, while affirming the spiritual power and effects of the ceremony. Yet it is this more rigorous "faith alone" understanding of justification and the literal presence of Jesus in the Lord's Supper that give Lutheranism its distinctiveness (Dayton and Johnston, 222-244).

"Adventist Essentials" Identified—What gives Adventism its special, distinctive flavor? What are those essentials that, if one took them away, would leave Adventism theologically emasculated? What are those doctrines that, taken together, have given us our theological identity?

I would suggest the following: the second coming of Jesus as literal, visible, cataclysmic, imminent, posttribulation, and premillennial; the millennium as a distinct period coming between the Second Coming and the final executionary judgment of the wicked and the setting up of the everlasting earthly kingdom; the application of "historicist" as opposed to "preterist" and "futurist" principles of prophetic interpretation (especially in the study of the books of Daniel and Revelation); the eternal and universal authority of the law of God; the seventh-day Sabbath as a moral requirement for New Testament Christians and the eschatological sign of trusting and obedient Christians in the last days; the sanctuary and pre-Advent judgment teaching, with its emphasis on Christ as our high priestly advocate, judge, justifier, and sanctifier; the understanding of human nature, especially as this interpretation points to the importance of physical health, the conditional nature of immortality, and the utter annihilation of the wicked; and the "formative"[11] theological influence of Ellen White as an authoritative prophet of God. These, I would suggest, are the distinctive essentials of Adventism.

They are the truths that have stood the test of time and been expounded with a strong consensus in our journals and books, have been proclaimed by our pastors and evangelists, and are supported by Ellen White.

Ellen White and the Essentials

In reference to Ellen White, I would suggest that she supported all of the above-listed essentials. She, however, advocated an even more limited listing of the essentials, or landmarks.

In the crisis-laden atmosphere of 1888, facing the charge that the new emphasis on justification by faith would do away with the landmarks, Ellen White gave a rather terse definition of distinctive Adventism. Referring to "the cleansing of the sanctuary in heaven," its "decided relation to God's people on the earth," and the three angels' messages, she declared that "one of the landmarks under this message was the temple of God, seen by His truth-loving people in heaven, and the ark containing the law of God. The light of the Sabbath of the fourth commandment flashed its strong rays in the pathway of the transgressors of God's law. The nonimmortality of the wicked is an old landmark. I can call to mind nothing more that can come under the head of the old landmarks. All this cry about changing the old landmarks is all imaginary" (CWE 30, 31).

I find it instructive that when Ellen White found herself in a crisis atmosphere regarding the issues of righteousness by faith, facing charges that the justificationist emphasis was endangering the pillars and the landmarks, she could in response only suggest a few issues that were the distinctive essentials of Adventism. She was even more succinct in her listing of landmarks than I have been in suggesting the essentials.

The Implications for Historic Adventism

Would it be fair to conclude that when we get into disagreements about righteousness by faith (and closely related issues such as the humanity of Christ), we need to be cautious about questioning the legitimacy of the Adventist credentials of any person who might have a differing perspective?

Taken as a whole, these essentials have given Adventism a clearly identifiable theological cast that is uniquely its own. Some of these points we share with others, some are quite uniquely our own, but taken together they make Seventh-day Adventism "essentially" Adventist!

Is it asking too much to agree that all who affirm these essentials can be called Adventist despite differing perspectives on issues related to righteousness by faith and the more distinctive understandings of Christ's humanity? I would suggest that within this suggested framework of essential Adventism, standing on the platform of the great eternal verities that we share with most Bible-affirming Christians (especially Protestants), we have plenty of room to move and develop theologically without having to engage in divisive doctrinal jousts.

If one affirms these essentials, it would seem that there ought to be room enough to discuss, even vigorously dialogue about, controverted "processive" issues.

The Humanity of Christ: A Suggested Approach

How, then, should we approach such an issue as the humanity of Christ?

I would suggest that we should begin with a realistic hope that the issue can be resolved! With the history of how we have come to clarity over the Arian issue, the time to commence the Sabbath, the "law in Galatians," and Systematic Benevolence, we can be at least moderately optimistic about finding resolution on this processive issue. Such resolution will not come, though, unless we are willing to grant some breathing room within the framework of essential Adventism.

Before offering some questions about and tentative solutions to the issues of Christology, I would like to remind us of some simple procedural methods that should prove helpful in resolving theological disagreements.[12]

Procedural Methods—First, we need to cultivate a prayerful, humble, and teachable spirit; be willing to give up a cherished opinion, esteeming others better than ourselves; and have a spirit of openness to God's unfolding light.

Second, we should listen carefully and charitably to what our partners in theological dialogue are saying.

Third, we should state any position clearly, but humbly, seeking to give partners in dialogue every respect for their position.

And last, partners in theological dialogue should find agreement on as many points as possible. Let's seek the common ground before moving into controverted quicksand.

Basic Suggestions and Questions to Ponder—What I am suggesting in the following paragraphs is a preliminary theological agenda for earnest dialogue aimed at reconciling some of the divisions within Adventism. It is not meant to be an exhaustive or final treatment of the issues themselves.

Clearly Christology and perfection (and their deep interrelatedness) are the undergirding issues that drive most doctrinal discussions that deeply concern historic Adventists. Essential Adventists of every hue should affirm historic Adventism's desire to exalt the humanity of Jesus and its emphasis on His identity with fallen sinners. Historic Adventists have been correct in giving this aspect of Christology an emphasis it so richly deserves and in recognizing that both the Bible and Ellen White give this theme due attention, attention often sadly lacking in the Christian tradition. We can heartily affirm that Jesus has a profound identity with our fallen humanity and has certainly experienced our "infirmities."

Other sincere Adventists, however, have had some deep reservations about the so-called post-Fall position because it has raised some troubling questions in their minds.

Some Questions for "Historics" to Ponder—In all of the zeal to emphasize His identity, has there not been a tendency to seek simplistic and dogmatic expressions of mysteries that have challenged Christian thinkers for 2,000 years? Has there not been a tendency to neglect the understanding that, from birth, Jesus had to be sinless in nature as well as in actions if He is to be both a victorious helper and a fully sinless and effective substitute? Can Jesus really be our justifying substitute if He is just like us in nature? Could Jesus, who never sinned once, be exactly like us, when we have engaged in all sorts of "habitual" sin? Does not repetitive sin deepen its hold on us to a greater extent than it does over a person who has never once indulged?

Could it be that the view of sin espoused by the post-Fall advocates is too superficial? Is not sin more than just bad actions and poor choices? Isn't it also the fruit of a profoundly deranged nature steeped in a selfishness that "is inwrought in our very being" and that "has come to us as an inheritance" (HS 138, 139)? If Jesus was just like us, are we prepared to declare that He was "naturally depraved" and "born with inherent propensities of disobedience," both expressions Ellen White applies to sinners but never to Jesus (IHP 163; 5BC 1128)? Again I ask: Could Jesus really be just like us in nature and still be our sinless substitute?

What of the epochal Baker letter? Are we really to believe that when Ellen White says that we are never to "leave the slightest impression upon human minds that a taint of, or inclination to, corruption rested upon Christ" (QOD 652) she means only that He did not give in to temptation? What does she mean when she admonishes that "every human being be warned from the ground of making Christ altogether human, such an one as ourselves; for it cannot be" (ibid.)? Has there not been a tendency to ignore, even twist, the obvious meaning of contrary evidence from the writings of Ellen White?

In the light of such evidence from the Bible and the pen of Ellen White that appears problematic to the post-Fall position, would it be possible for one to hold a post-Fall view as a matter of processive opinion and not absolutely essential Adventist orthodoxy? Could we all apply the following to ourselves?

"God and heaven alone are infallible. Those who think that they will never have to give up a cherished view, never have occasion to change an opinion, will be disappointed. As long as we hold to our own ideas and opinions with determined persistency, we cannot have the unity for which Christ prayed" (CWE 37).

Nobody is asking anyone to give up any views because of coercion, but could they be held as sincere personal opinion without being divisive and judgmental?

Would it be enough to profess something like the following?

Jesus was sufficiently like us in nature (a deep *identity*) to really be able to identify with our struggles in temptation and give us every victory needed to make it through to the kingdom, and yet also is sufficiently unlike us (a profound *uniqueness*) to be sinless enough in nature and performance to be our fully satisfactory, sinless substitute.

Again, I must emphasize that I have not attempted to be thorough or comprehensive in addressing the nature of Christ, but this is the type of questioning dialogue that I would suggest could help us out of the present impasse. We should say much more about issues that trouble sincere historic Adventists, but I trust that we have only just begun.

How Shall We Proceed?

First, I would urge that we start with all charity and patience by seeking to be as affirming of one another as we possibly can. With firmness of conviction, tempered with much listening and deep sympathy, progress can be made.

Second, I would urge that the expression "historic Adventism" has become so controversial that we need new expressions and a more inclusive theological framework and atmosphere if we are to find some resolution to the present, divisive impasse.

I would therefore urge that we lay aside such phrases as "historic Adventism," "traditional Adventism," and "new theology"[13] as divisive buzzwords and needless red flags that bring neither constructive doctrinal resolution nor accurate historical insight.

Is it possible to lay aside such derogatory expressions now, seek the common ground of essential Adventism, and proceed with all humility, charity, and honesty to the dialogue on processive Adventism? One of my deepest longings is that historic Adventists will answer my appeal affirmatively and that believers who do not share their particular burdens will be open, charitable, accepting, and patient in Christian respect. In the grace of Jesus I am optimistic that this impasse can be broken and that the Advent movement can more efficiently and unitedly get on with its mission!

---

[1] This chapter is an edited version of an article that appeared in the October 1993 *Ministry* entitled "Essential Adventism or Historic Adventism?"

[2] These persons especially see the treatment of these issues in the publication of *Questions on Doctrine* as taking a tragically sinister and compromising direction.

[3] For a recent example of the use of such terminology, see *Our Firm Foundation* 7, No. 3 (1992): 2-7.

[4] See *Questions on Doctrine*, pp. 21-25.

[5] See *Selected Messages*, book 1, pp. 169-175. Because of the limited space and their relative lack of importance, I will not include a discussion of nonessentials.

[6] For more background on Adventist doctrinal development, see Schwarz's *Light Bearers to the Remnant*, especially pp. 166-182.

[7] Professor C. Mervyn Maxwell also has an excellent discussion of Adventist Arianism in A. V. Wallenkampf

and W. Richard Lesher's *The Sanctuary and the Atonement*, pp. 530-533.

[8] The reader is urged to ponder carefully the wonderful facsimile collection of Ellen White's comments on 1888 in the four volumes of *The Ellen White 1888 Materials*.

[9] For further background and discussion of this issue, see Whidden, *Ellen White on Salvation*, pp. 87-98.

[10] I am indebted to Richard Schwarz for these terms. See his discussion in *Light Bearers*, pp. 393-407.

[11] I am using the expression "formative" quite technically in relationship to the more final and authoritative technical expression "normative." Adventism has always held to the Bible and the Bible alone as the ultimate normative standard of faith and practice, but it has also affirmed that Ellen White's counsels and theological insights have pointed the way and confirmed biblical truth. Yet we have always held that her definitions must ultimately be subject to biblical evidence. This use of Ellen White is in marked contrast to the Mormon attitude toward the writings of Joseph Smith or Christian Science's use of Mary Baker Eddy.

[12] See *Counsels to Writers and Editors*, pp. 29-54, for the basic source of the following suggestions.

[13] In a quick look at the published writings of Ellen G. White on compact disc, I was unable to locate a single instance in which she employed these terms.

CHAPTER ELEVEN

"The Lower and Higher Natures: The Key to Resolving the Adventist Christology Debate"

by Kevin Paulson

oodrow Whidden claims at one point that "for Ellen White, 'nature' usually refers to a person's inheritance, or what he or she is 'naturally' born with" (p. 34). Here is a serious understatement, but nevertheless one that touches the key by which we can settle this entire controversy.

The Bible is clear that both lower and higher forces exist in human nature. Jesus declared, "The spirit indeed is willing, but the flesh is weak" (Matt. 26:41). Paul spoke of bringing his body into subjection (1 Cor. 9:27). Contrary to what some have alleged, this has nothing to do with the body/soul dualism of Greek or popular Christian thought, nor is it related in any way to what happens to people when they die. While Seventh-day Adventists teach a wholistic view of human nature, we cannot deny the inspired truth that different forces exist within human beings.

Ellen White clearly makes this distinction: "The will is not the taste or the inclination, but it is the deciding power" (5T 513). In numerous statements she describes the need for the lower passions to remain subject to the higher powers of the being (MH 130; CH 41, 42; 5T 335; COL 354; RH, Dec. 1, 1896; AH 127, 128; MYP 237).

In one of the above statements she makes it clear that the lower, fleshly nature is of itself not capable of sinning: "The lower passions have their seat in the body and work through it. The words 'flesh' or 'fleshly' or 'carnal lusts' embrace the lower, corrupt nature; the flesh of itself cannot act contrary to the will of God. We are commanded to crucify the flesh, with the affections and lusts" (AH 127, 128).

Once we understand this distinction between the lower and higher natures, we can better understand the two types of Ellen White statements on passions and propensities relative to human beings, as well as the two types of statements relative to the humanity of Christ.

Whidden quotes a number of Ellen White statements that say Jesus did not possess the same passions and propensities (tendencies) to sin as we ourselves (2T 201, 202, 509; 5BC 1128; 16MR 182), as well as others that say clearly that He did (Ms. 73, 1892 [partially cited in IHP 155]; ST, Apr. 9, 1896; Oct. 17, 1900). He claims that the passions described in the latter group of statements "probably referred to normal human desires, appetites, feelings, or emotions rather than perverted desires that naturally tend to break over the bounds of lawful expression" (pp. 53, 54).

But a careful look at the statements, both on the surface and in context, makes it clear that his interpretation is not possible. Ironically, Whidden quotes enough of the context of the statement from manuscript 73, 1892, to demolish his own argument. Listen to Ellen White's words: "If you indulge in a nasty spirit, and give utterance to passionate words and foolish talk, you bring forth from the treasure of the heart evil things."

Then she says of Christ: "Though He had all the strength and passion of humanity, never did He yield to temptation to do one single act which was not pure and elevating and ennobling" (*ibid.*).

Elsewhere she comments: "The words of Christ encourage parents to bring their little ones to Jesus. They may be wayward, and possess passions like those of humanity, but this should not deter us from bringing them to Christ. He blessed children that were possessed of passions *like His own*" (ST, Apr. 9, 1896; italics supplied).

It is utterly impossible for Whidden to explain away these statements as referring to "normal human desires" rather than "perverted desires" (pp. 53, 54). We read here of the spirit of hastiness, evil things concealed in the treasure of the heart (in this case the lower nature), and that while Jesus had all the strength of such passions, He never yielded to the temptation to do anything impure, degrading, or ignoble. When she speaks of children blessed by Jesus possessing passions "like His own," and in the previous sentence talks about our children being "wayward" with "passions like those of humanity," what kind of passions could she possibly be referring to except perverted ones? Would the sinless, unperverted passions of Adam and Eve in our children be likely to deter us from bringing them to Christ?

How, then, do we harmonize these statements with those that clearly deny that Jesus had our passions and propensities to sin? By understanding the principle we have already established from Scripture and Ellen White—that of the lower and higher natures. When Ellen White says He had our passions, she is talking about the lower nature, which of itself cannot sin (AH 127). But when she says He did not have our passions, she is referring to the higher nature, which involves the will and behavioral choices.

This is more clearly explained when we find statements that speak of the need to "cast out" evil passions (DA 305); that "as we partake of the divine nature, hereditary and cultivated tendencies to wrong are cut away from the character"; and that "we need not retain one sinful propensity" (7BC 943; see also TM 171, 172; MYP 42). Notice that she describes these tendencies as being cut away from the *character* (higher nature), not from the flesh (lower nature). Clearly, when she speaks of evil passions cast out and sinful propensities not retained, she is not teaching "holy flesh," since we read elsewhere, "Appetite and passion must be brought under the control of the Holy Spirit. There is no end to the warfare this side of eternity" (CT 20).

In his effort to prove that our inherited sinful nature is the same as sin itself, Whidden repeatedly cites one of the most commonly distorted Ellen White statements in the current Adventist salvation controversy, from *Selected Messages,* book 1, page 344 (see also FW 23, 24; Whidden cites this on pages 23, 24, 64, 65, 88, 89). In these statements Ellen White says the words and deeds even of true believers are so defiled by their corrupt human channels that they need purification by Christ's blood. Whidden implies that this is a forensic purification thrown over our actions as soon as they arrive in the heavenly sanctuary, since original sin has supposedly polluted even sanctified behavior.

But other Ellen White statements using the same or similar language as *Selected Messages*, book 1, page 344, make it clear that this is not a forensic purification applied to the books of heaven, but an internal purification directed from heaven but taking place in the heart and life. She states that "man's obedience can be made perfect only by the incense of Christ's righteousness, *which fills with divine fragrance every act of obedience*" (AA 532; italics supplied; see also 7BC 909; ChS 263; IHP 72).

Quite obviously, the process here described is not forensic, but internal. Our prayers and praise and obedience ascend through the corrupt channels of our fallen natures to the heavenly sanctuary, but it is *while* they ascend through those channels—not when they get to heaven—that they receive purification.

Twice Whidden asks whether Jesus could be our saving, sacrificial substitute and still be called "depraved," corrupt, and be characterized as having natural propensities and tendencies to sin—a "bent" to evil (p. 22; see also pp. 87, 88). Whidden firmly answers no! (pp. 22, 89). But Ellen White firmly answers yes (Ms. 73, 1892; ST, Apr. 9, 1896; Oct. 17, 1900; 4BC 1147). Such tendencies and passions remained confined to His lower, fleshly nature, which of itself is incapable of sin (AH 127). He never permitted the lower passions and propensities to possess His higher nature. And the glorious truth of Scripture and Ellen White, enshrined at the heart of classic Adventism, is that through His power the fleshly nature may be subdued in us, as it was in Him (Rom. 8:3, 4), and His sinless life reproduced in ours. In closing:

"The Saviour is wounded afresh and put to open shame when His people pay no need to His word. He came to this world and lived a sinless life, that in His power His people might also live lives of sinlessness" (RH, April 1, 1902).

Reply to Paulson

Kevin Paulson has raised a very important issue in his proposed distinction between the "lower and higher natures" of Christ. His interpretation clearly maintains that Christ had a "lower" nature that included "perverted desires." He claims that it is "utterly impossible . . . to explain away" the statements I cite as referring only to "normal human desires." I, however, find his interpretation hanging on a very thin thread of evidence.

I must confess that part of the problem with one of Paulson's key pieces of evidence is how I originally cited the statement from manuscript 73, 1892, in Appendix B of the original manuscript draft of this book. When I found a copy of the original manuscript 73, 1892, in its full context, I discovered the following:

The first part of the statement that speaks of a "hasty spirit," giving "utterance to passionate words and foolish talk," and bringing "from the treasure of the heart evil things" (1) is not explicitly applied to Christ and (2) is separated contextually by more than a page from the statement that declares that Christ "had all the strength and passion of humanity." When we read these statements in the context of the total flow of the manuscript, it is certainly stretching it to imply (and it is only an implication) that Jesus had "the spirit of hastiness, foolishness, [and] evil things concealed in the treasure of the heart."[1]

Paulson's second piece of evidence, taken from *Signs of the Times*, April 9, 1896, is a bit more persuasive; but once again, his interpretation is also only an implication. The statement is not explicit in declaring that Jesus possessed "passions like those of humanity" (and Paulson implies that Christ's passions were *just* "like" or *exactly identical* to ours).

Furthermore, if I used the same interpretive method for this passage as Paulson does, I could imply that Jesus' passions made Him "wayward." Now, I do not impute this interpretation to Paulson, since we both know that there are too many Ellen White statements denying that Jesus was in any instance "wayward." All I am suggesting is that Ellen White also has some clear statements that reject the idea that Jesus' passions were just like or exactly identical to ours—as Paulson wants to suggest by implication from the passage in question.

The manner in which Paulson (or anyone, myself included) draws implications about the nature of Christ needs to be employed very judiciously, and we must take the whole of what Ellen White says into account. This is especially necessary in interpreting the statement in question. In other more explicit statements she declared that "it is not correct to say, as many writers have said, that Christ was like all children. He was not like all children." In the same paragraph she then went on to say that "His inclination to right was a constant gratification to His parents." Three paragraphs later she said that "no one, looking upon the childlike countenance, shining with animation, could say that Christ was just like other children" (YI, Sept. 8, 1898).

If I applied Paulson's implied interpretive methods to the apostle Paul's statement in Romans 8:3 that God sent Jesus "in the likeness of sinful flesh," I could easily come up with the following interpretation: Since the context of the immediately preceding Romans 7 speaks of someone who is "carnal, sold under sin"—who does not do what they know they should do and then actually does what they "hate"—I could conclude that Jesus, in the "likeness of sinful flesh," was actually "sold under sin" in the sense of neglecting the good and doing what He "hated." Do we really want to interpret Scripture and Ellen White to imply such things about Jesus? I think not.

I would suggest that a better interpretation of Jesus' "higher and lower natures" appears on pages 48-51 in this book. The "lower nature" of Jesus included normal passions and appetites that were weakened by the effects of sin, but not *infected* with such sin that made them perverted, inherently evil, and corrupt. Certainly the "higher nature" of Jesus included His "will and behavioral choices," but it also involved a lack of infective perversion.

Paulson's treatment of the quotation from *Selected Messages*, book 1, page 344, is interesting, but disregards the statement's clear declaration that the righteous acts *"ascend* from true believers . . . to the heavenly sanctuary. . . . They *ascend* not in spotless purity," but are purified by "the Intercessor, *who is at God's right hand.*" This "Intercessor," who is *"before the Father,"* gathers into the "censer of His own merits" the righteous acts of "true believers." "Then, perfumed with the merits of Christ's propitiation, the incense comes up before God wholly and entirely acceptable" (italics supplied). It is very clear from the context that all of this purification takes place in heaven, and is not "an internal purification . . . taking place in the heart and life."

What Paulson has done is go to other Ellen White statements dealing with sanctification in believers; and since a number of these statements use such expressions as "the incense of Christ's righteousness," Paulson then makes the facile assumption that such "sanctificationist" applications must then explain every other Ellen White usage of such expressions. This is not good interpretation.

Ellen White does use the terminology of *Selected Messages*, book 1, page 344, in sanctificationist, perfectionist settings, but that does not deny the clear application of this terminology to the justificationist, intercessory work of Christ for "true believers"—in heaven (a similar, forceful example of this appears in the *Review and Herald*, of Mar. 1, 1892). It is not one application swallowing up another, but both expressing different though essential effects of the "incense of Christ's righteousness."

I am clear that Paulson understands that forensic righteousness covers the sins of the past for penitent sinners. But Paulson's interpretation of *Selected Messages*, book 1, page 344, certainly causes one to question whether his Christology has driven him to deny almost totally any forensic, objective, justifying ministry by Christ in heaven to atone for the corrupting influences of believers' sinful natures on their "sanctified successes."[2] Maybe the question could be put another way: after initial forgiveness, is the basis or ground of our acceptance with God some sort of good works produced by divinely infused merit?[3]

—Woodrow Whidden III

---

[1] Furthermore, it should be noted that manuscript 73, 1892, is a portion of a letter to Edson White (letter 27, 1892). The letter and its first published version (in ST, Nov. 21, 1892) read "If you indulge in slang phrases and foolish talk" rather than in indulging in "a hasty spirit" and giving "utterance to passionate words." In other words, Ellen White added the expression "passionate words" to the manuscript. Manuscript 73, 1892, as revised by Ellen White, is what I have cited in Appendix B of this book.

[2] This expression, "sanctified successes," is Paulson's own, used in personal correspondence with me on this issue.

[3] I wonder what the reader's answer to this question might be. In his personal correspondence with me Paulson has been forthright in his answer to this very question: "On the basis of both Scripture and Ellen White, the answer is an emphatic yes! And down into a grave of dishonor goes a cherished icon of contemporary Adventism!" I wonder how other post-Fall partisans feel about the conclusions that Paulson's Christology has led him to. Could it be that Paulson has followed his post-Fall presuppositions on the nature of Christ to their logical implications?

Section 5

THE PRIMARY ELLEN WHITE DOCUMENTS

Ellen White on "Depravity and Sin"

In Heavenly Places, pp. 195, 196 (originally from letter 26d, 1887): "Bad habits are more easily formed than good habits, and the bad habits are given up with more difficulty. The natural depravity of the heart accounts for this well-known fact—that it takes far less labor to demoralize the youth, to corrupt their ideas of moral and religious character, than to engraft upon their character the enduring, pure, and uncorrupted habits of righteousness and truth. . . . In our present fallen state all that is needed is to give up the mind and character to its natural tendencies. . . .

"The moral dangers to which all, both old and young, are exposed are daily increasing. Moral derangement, which we call depravity, finds ample room to work, and an influence is exerted by men, women, and youth professing to be Christians that is low, sensual, devilish."

Selected Messages, book 1, p. 310: "No man inherits holiness as a birthright."

Education, p. 15: "Through sin the divine likeness was marred, and well-nigh obliterated. Man's physical powers were weakened, his mental capacity was lessened, his spiritual vision dimmed."

Education, pp. 28, 29: "Sin not only shuts us away from God, but destroys in the human soul both the desire and the capacity for knowing Him. All this work of evil it is Christ's mission to undo. The faculties of the soul, paralyzed by sin, the darkened mind, the perverted will, He has power to invigorate and to restore. . . .

"Not only intellectual but spiritual power, a perception of right, a desire for goodness, exists in every heart. But against these principles there is struggling an antagonistic power. The result of the eating of the tree of knowledge of good and evil is manifest in every man's experience. There is in his nature a bent to evil, a force which, unaided, he cannot resist. . . . He can find help in but one power. That power is Christ."

Testimonies for the Church, vol. 5, p. 645: "God will be better glorified if we confess the secret, inbred corruption of the heart to Jesus alone."

The Desire of Ages, p. 161: "Because of sin, humanity ceased to be a temple for God. Darkened and defiled by evil, the heart of man no longer revealed the glory of the Divine One."

The Desire of Ages, p. 172: "The fountain of the heart must be purified before the streams can become pure. . . . The Christian's life is not a modification or improvement of the old, but a transformation of nature."

Steps to Christ, p. 62: "It was possible for Adam, before the Fall, to form a righteous character by obedience to God's law. But he failed to do this, and because of his sin our natures are fallen and we cannot make ourselves righteous. Since we are sinful, unholy, we cannot perfectly obey the holy law. We have no righteousness of our own with which to meet the claims of the law of God. But Christ has made a way of escape for us."

Seventh-day Adventist Bible Commentary, vol. 5, p. 1128 (letter 8, 1895 [this is the famous Baker letter]): "The first Adam was created a pure, sinless being, without a taint of sin upon him; he was in the image of God. He could fall, and he did fall through transgressing. Because of sin his posterity was born with inherent propensities of disobedience."

Signs of the Times, Nov. 15, 1883: "Christ brought His divinity to earth, veiled by humanity, in order to rescue man from his lost condition.

Human nature is vile, and man's character must be changed before it can harmonize with the pure and holy in God's immortal kingdom. This transformation is the new birth."

Review and Herald, May 27, 1884: "There was no sin in Him that Satan could triumph over, no weakness or defect that he could use to His advantage. But we are sinful by nature, and we have a work to do to cleanse the soul-temple of every defilement."

Patriarchs and Prophets, p. 61: "The sin of our first parents brought guilt and sorrow upon the world, and had it not been for the goodness and mercy of God, would have plunged the race into hopeless despair. . . . They [Adam and Eve] were told that their nature had become depraved by sin; they had lessened their strength to resist evil and had opened the way for Satan to gain more ready access to them. In their innocence they had yielded to temptation; and now, in a state of conscious guilt, they would have less power to maintain their integrity."

Patriarchs and Prophets, p. 306: "It is inevitable that children should suffer from the consequences of parental wrongdoing, but they are not punished for the parents' guilt, except as they participate in their sins. It is usually the case, however, that children walk in the steps of their parents."

Patriarchs and Prophets, p. 371: "Living in the midst of idolatry and corruption, they [the children of Israel at the Exodus] had no true conception of the holiness of God, of the exceeding sinfulness of their own hearts, their utter inability, in themselves, to render obedience to God's law, and their need of a Saviour."

Historical Sketches, pp. 138, 139: "There is a great work to be done for many of us. Our minds and characters must become as the mind and character of Christ. Selfishness is inwrought in our very being. It has come to us as an inheritance, and has been cherished by many as a precious treasure. No special work for God can be accomplished until self and selfishness are overcome. To many everything connected with themselves is of great importance. Self is a center, around which everything seems to revolve."

Selected Messages, book 1, p. 344: "The religious services, the prayers, the praise, the penitent confession of sin ascend from true believers as incense to the heavenly sanctuary, but passing through the corrupt channels of humanity, they are so defiled that unless purified by blood, they can never be of value with God. . . . Unless the Intercessor, who is at God's right hand, presents and purifies all by His righteousness, it is not acceptable to God. All incense from earthly tabernacles must be moist with the cleansing drops of the blood of Christ. He holds before the Father the censer of His own merits, in which there is no taint of earthly corruption. . . .

"Oh, that all may see that everything in obedience, in penitence, in praise and thanksgiving, must be placed upon the glowing fire of the righteousness of Christ."

Faith and Works, pp. 23, 24 (taken from manuscript 36, 1890): "There must be nothing less given than duty prescribes, and there cannot be one jot more given than they have first received; and all must be laid upon the fire of Christ's righteousness to cleanse it from its earthly odor before it rises in a cloud of fragrant incense to the great Jehovah and is accepted as a sweet savor. . . .

"If you would gather together everything that is good and holy and noble and lovely in man and then present the subject to the angels of God as acting a part in the salvation of the human soul or in merit, the proposition would be rejected as treason. . . .

"And any works that man can render to God will be far less than nothingness. My requests are made acceptable only because they are laid upon Christ's righteousness."

In Heavenly Places, p. 146: "As a result of Adam's disobedience every human being is a transgressor of the law, sold under sin."

In Heavenly Places, p. 163 (compare *Counsels to Parents, Teachers, and Students*, p. 544): "In order to understand the matter aright, we must remember that our hearts are naturally depraved, and we are unable of ourselves to pursue a right course. It is only by the grace of God, combined with the most earnest effort on our part, that we can gain the victory."

That I May Know Him, p. 136: "We should remember that our own ways are not faultless. We make mistakes again and again. . . . No one is perfect but Jesus."

Child Guidance, p. 475 (taken from letter 68, 1899, and also cited in *The Seventh-day Adventist Bible Commentary*, vol. 6, p. 1074): "The inheritance of children is that of sin. Sin has separated them from God. Jesus gave His life that He might unite the broken links to God. As related to the first Adam, men receive from him nothing but guilt and the sentence of death."

Letter 10, 1888 (cf. *E. G. White Manuscript Releases*, vol. 8, p. 208): "One of the deplorable effects of the original apostasy was the loss of man's power to govern his own heart. When there is a separation from the Source of your strength, when you are lifted up in pride, you cannot but transgress the law of your moral constitution."

Manuscript 60, 1905 (cf. *E. G. White Manuscript Releases*, vol. 8, p. 210): "We are not to seek to extenuate the consequences of the original apostasy. It is not possible to overstate the degree of alienation from truth and righteousness entered into by those whose souls revolt from God."

Review and Herald, Dec. 17, 1872: "Man could not atone for man. His sinful, fallen condition would constitute him an imperfect offering, an atoning sacrifice of less value than Adam before his fall. God made man perfect and upright, and after his transgression there could be no sacrifice acceptable to God for him, unless the offering made should in value be superior to man as he was in his state of perfection and innocency."

Signs of the Times, May 19, 1890: "Adam sinned, and the children of Adam share his guilt and its consequences; but Jesus bore the guilt of Adam, and all the children of Adam that will flee to Christ, the second Adam, may escape the penalty of transgression."

Counsels to Parents, Teachers, and Students, p. 20: "There are hereditary and cultivated tendencies to evil that must be overcome."

Review and Herald, Apr. 16, 1901: "Through the medium of influence, taking advantage of the action of mind on mind, he prevailed on Adam to sin. Thus at its very source human nature was corrupted. And ever since then sin has continued its hateful work, reaching mind to mind. Every sin committed awakens the echoes of the original sin."

Seventh-day Adventist Bible Commentary, vol. 1, p. 1083 (letter 191, 1899): "In what consisted the strength of the assault made upon Adam, which caused his fall? It was not indwelling sin; for God made Adam after His own character, pure and upright. There were no corrupt principles in the first Adam, no corrupt propensities or tendencies to evil. Adam was as faultless as the angels before God's throne. These things are inexplainable."

APPENDIX B

Ellen White on the Humanity of Christ

1858:

Spiritual Gifts, vol. 1, p. 25: "Jesus also told them . . . that He should take man's fallen nature, and His strength would not be even equal with theirs."

1863:

Review and Herald, Jan. 20, 1863: "I saw that Jesus knows our infirmities, and Himself hath felt their experiences in all things but in sin, therefore He hath proportioned a way and a path to our strength and capacity, and like Jacob, hath marched softly and in evenness with the children as they were able to endure."

1864:

Spiritual Gifts, vol. 4a, p. 115: "It was in the order of God that Christ should take upon Himself the form and nature of fallen man."

Spiritual Gifts, vol. 4a, p. 119: "When the Son of God came into the world to die [as] man's sacrifice, He laid aside His glory and exalted stature. His height was but a little above the general size of men. His personal appearance bore no special marks of His divine character, which would of itself inspire faith. Yet His perfect form, and dignified bearing, His countenance expressing benevolence, love and holiness, were unequaled by any then living upon the earth."

1868:

Testimonies for the Church, vol. 2, pp. 508, 509: "He was unsullied with corruption, a stranger to sin; yet He prayed, and that often with strong crying and tears. He prayed for His disciples and for Himself, thus identifying Himself with our needs, our weaknesses, and our failings, which are so common with humanity. He was a mighty petitioner, not possessing the passions of our human, fallen natures, but compassed with like infirmities, tempted in all points even as we are. Jesus endured agony which required help and support from His Father."

1869:

Testimonies for the Church, vol. 2, pp. 201, 202 (cf. *Signs of the Times*, Aug. 7, 1879): "Taking human nature fitted Christ to understand man's trials and sorrows, and all the temptations wherewith he is beset. Angels who were unacquainted with sin could not sympathize with man in his peculiar trials. Christ condescended to take man's nature and was tempted in all points like as we, that He might know how to succor all who should be tempted.

"As the human was upon Him, He felt His need of strength from His Father. He had select places of prayer. He loved to hold communion with His Father. . . . In this exercise His holy, human soul was strengthened for the duties and trials of the day. Our Saviour identifies Himself with our needs and weaknesses, in that He became a suppliant, a nightly petitioner, seeking from His Father fresh supplies of strength, to come forth invigorated and refreshed, braced for duty and trial. He is our example in all things. He is a brother in our infirmities, but not in possessing like passions. As the sinless One, His nature recoiled from evil. He endured struggles and torture of soul in a world of sin. His humanity made prayer a necessity and privilege."

1870:

Review and Herald, Apr. 19, 1870: "The great burden-bearer, who took our nature that He might understand how to sympathize with our frailty, and with our temptations, knows how to succor those that are tempted.

And does He say, Carry your burdens yourself? No; but, Come unto me ye that are weary and heavy laden, and I will give you rest."

Review and Herald, May 31, 1870: "Christ humiliated Himself to humanity, and took upon Himself our natures, that . . . He might become a stepping stone to fallen men, that they might climb up upon His merits, and through His excellence and virtue receive from God an acceptance of their efforts to keep His law."

"Christ steps in between fallen man and God, and says to man, You may yet come to the Father."

1872:

Review and Herald, Dec. 17, 1872: "Man could not atone for man. His sinful, fallen condition would constitute him an imperfect offering, an atoning sacrifice of less value than Adam before his fall. God made man perfect and upright, and after his transgression there could be no sacrifice acceptable to God for him, unless the offering made should in value be superior to man as he was in his state of perfection and innocency.

"The divine Son of God was the only sacrifice of sufficient value to fully satisfy the claims of God's perfect law. . . .

"Christ alone could open the way, by making an offering equal to the demands of the divine law. He was perfect, and undefiled by sin. He was without spot or blemish."

Review and Herald, Dec. 24, 1872: "This was the reception the Saviour met when He came to a fallen world. He . . . took upon Himself man's nature, that He might save the fallen race. Instead of men glorifying God for the honor He had conferred upon them in thus sending His Son in the likeness of sinful flesh, . . ."

Review and Herald, Dec. 31, 1872: "It was in the order of God that Christ should take upon Himself the form and nature of fallen man, that He might be made perfect through suffering, and Himself endure the strength of Satan's fierce temptations, that He might understand how to succor those who should be tempted."

1873:

Manuscript 3, 1873 (cf. *Manuscript Releases*, vol. 10, pp. 65, 66): "I then spoke upon Luke 21:34-36. I spoke of the sacrifice made by Christ for us and His bearing the test Adam failed to endure in Eden. He stood in Adam's place. He took humanity, and with divinity and humanity combined He could reach the race with His human arm while His divine arm grasped the Infinite. His name was the link which united man to God and God to man."

Youth's Instructor, February 1873 (cf. *Selected Messages*, book 3, pp. 133, 134): "Christ was our example in all things. He was a perfect pattern in childhood, in youth, and in manhood. . . .

"Christ, the Redeemer of the world, was not situated where the influences surrounding Him were the best calculated to preserve a life of purity and untainted morals, yet He was not contaminated. He was not free from temptation. Satan was earnest and persevering in his efforts to deceive and overcome the Son of God by his devices. Christ was the only one who walked the earth upon whom there rested no taint of sin. He was pure, spotless, and undefiled. That there should be One without the defilement of sin upon the earth greatly disturbed the author of sin, and he left no means untried to overcome Christ with his wily, deceptive power. But our Saviour relied upon His Heavenly Father for wisdom and strength to resist and overcome the tempter. . . . He was sinless. Virtue and purity characterized His life."

Youth's Instructor, April 1873 (cf. *Selected Messages*, book 3, p. 134): "Some may think that Christ, because He was the Son of God, did not have temptations as children now have. The Scriptures say He was tempted in all points like as we are tempted. And Satan made stronger attacks upon Christ than he will ever make upon us. . . .

[one paragraph later] "No, children, you can never be tempted in so determined and cruel a manner as was our Saviour. Satan was upon His path every moment. The strength of Christ was in prayer. He had taken humanity, and He bore our infirmities and became sin for us."

1874:

Review and Herald, Feb. 24, 1874: "Through His humiliation and poverty Christ would identify Himself with the weaknesses of the fallen race. . . .

"The great work of redemption could be carried out only by the Redeemer taking the place of fallen Adam. . . .

"The King of glory proposed to humble Himself to fallen humanity! . . . He would take man's fallen nature and engage to cope with the strong foe who triumphed over Adam."

Review and Herald, July 28, 1874 (cf. *Selected Messages*, book 1, pp. 267, 268 and *Seventh-day Adventist Bible Commentary*, vol. 5, p. 1081; cf. *The Spirit of Prophecy*, vol. 2, p. 88, and *The Desire of Ages*, p. 117, for similar statements): "Christ was not in as favorable a position in the desolate wilderness to endure the temptations of Satan as was Adam when he was tempted in Eden. The Son of God humbled Himself and took man's nature after the race had wandered four thousand years from Eden, and from their original state of purity and uprightness. Sin had been making its terrible marks upon the race for ages; and physical, mental, and moral degeneracy prevailed throughout the human family.

"When Adam was assailed by the tempter in Eden he was without the taint of sin. . . .

"Christ, in the wilderness of temptation, stood in Adam's place to bear the test he failed to endure. Here Christ overcame in the sinner's behalf, four thousand years after Adam turned his back upon the light of his home. . . . The human family had been departing every successive generation, farther from the original purity, wisdom, and knowledge which Adam possessed in Eden. Christ bore the sins and infirmities of the race as they existed when He came to earth to help man. In behalf of the race, with the weaknesses of fallen man upon Him, He was to stand the temptations of Satan upon all points wherewith man would be assailed. . . .

"Adam was in the perfection of manhood, the noblest of the Creator's work. . . .

"In what contrast is the second Adam as He entered the gloomy wilderness to cope with Satan single-handed. Since the Fall the race had been decreasing in size and physical strength, and sinking lower in the scale of moral worth, up to the period of Christ's advent to the earth. And in order to elevate fallen man, Christ must reach him where he was. He took human nature, and bore the infirmities and degeneracy of the race. He, who knew no sin, became sin for us. He humiliated Himself to the lowest depths of human woe, that He might be qualified to reach man, and bring him up from the degradation in which sin had plunged him" (cf. 2 Tim. 3:13: "But evil men and seducers shall wax worse and worse").

Review and Herald, Aug. 4, 1874 (cf. *Selected Messages*, book 1, pp. 271ff.): "The weight of the sins of the world was pressing His soul, and His countenance expressed unutterable sorrow, a depth of anguish that fallen man had never realized. He felt the overwhelming tide of woe that deluged the world. He realized the strength of indulged appetite and of unholy passion that controlled the world. . . .

"The humanity of Christ reached to the very depths of human wretchedness, and identified itself with the weaknesses and necessities of fallen man, while His divine nature grasped the Eternal."

Review and Herald, Oct. 13, 1874: "Christ's humanity alone could never have endured this test [Satan's temptation in the wilderness], but His divine power combined with humanity gained in behalf of man an infinite victory. Our Representative in this victory raised humanity in the scale of moral value with God."

1875:
Review and Herald, Mar. 4, 1875: "Would that man had stopped falling with Adam. But there has been a succession of falls. . . .

"From Adam's day to ours there has been a succession of falls, each greater than the last, in every species of crime."

Review and Herald, Mar. 18, 1875: "He [Satan] put forth his strongest efforts to overcome Christ on the point of appetite at a time when He was enduring the keenest pangs of hunger. The victory gained was de-signed, not only to set an example to those who have fallen under the power of appetite, but to qualify the Redeemer for His special work of reaching to the very depths of human woe. By experiencing in Himself the strength of Satan's temptation, and of human sufferings and infirmities, He would know how to succor those who should put forth efforts to help themselves."

Review and Herald, Apr. 1, 1875: "If Christ had been deceived by Satan's temptations, and had exercised His miraculous power to relieve Himself from difficulty, He would have broken the contract made with His Father, to be a probationer in behalf of the race. . . .

"It was as difficult for Him to keep the level of humanity as it is for men to rise above the low level of their depraved natures, and be partakers of the divine nature.

"Christ was put to the closest test, requiring the strength of all His faculties to resist the inclination when in danger, to use His power to deliver Himself from peril, and triumph over the power of the prince of darkness. Satan showed his knowledge of the weak points of the human heart, and put forth his utmost power to take advantage of the weakness of the humanity which Christ had assumed in order to overcome His temptations on man's account. . . .

"Because the Son of God had linked Himself to the weakness of humanity, to be tempted in all points like as man should be tempted, Satan triumphed over Him, and taunted Him."

1877:

The Spirit of Prophecy, vol. 2, p. 39: "In Christ were united the human and the divine. . . . Taking human nature fitted Christ to understand the nature of man's trials, and all the temptations wherewith he is beset.

"Before Christ left Heaven and came into the world to die, He was taller than any of the angels. He was majestic and lovely. But when His ministry commenced, He was but little taller than the common size of men then living upon the earth. Had He come among men with His noble, heavenly form, His outward appearance would have attracted the minds of the people to Himself, and He would have been received without the exercise of faith.

"It was in the order of God that Christ should take upon Himself the form and nature of fallen man, that He might be made perfect through suffering, and Himself endure the strength of Satan's fierce temptations, that He might understand how to succor those who should be tempted."

P. 88: "Every enticement to evil, which men find so difficult to resist, was brought to bear upon the Son of God in as much greater degree as His character was superior to that of fallen man.

"When Adam was assailed by the tempter he was without the taint of sin. He stood before God in the strength of perfect manhood, all the organs and faculties of his being fully developed and harmoniously balanced. . . . What a contrast to this perfect being did the second Adam present, as He entered the desolate wilderness to cope with Satan, single-handed. For four thousand years the race had been decreasing in size and physical strength, and deteriorating in moral worth; and, in order to elevate fallen man, Christ must reach him where he stood. He assumed human nature, bearing the infirmities and degeneracy of the race. He humiliated Himself to the lowest depths of human woe, that He might fully sympathize with man and rescue him from the degradation into which sin had plunged him."

Signs of the Times, Jan. 4, 1877: "He had taken upon Himself the form of humanity with all its attendant ills."

1878:

Letter 17, 1878 (cf. *Manuscript Releases*, vol. 20, p. 71; *Our High Calling*, p. 57): "I present before you the great Exemplar. . . . As really did He meet and resist the temptations of Satan as any of the children of humanity. In this sense alone could He be a perfect example for man. He subjected Himself to humanity to become acquainted with all the temptations wherewith man is beset. He took upon Him the infirmities and bore the sorrow of the sons of Adam.

"He was 'made like unto his brethren' (Heb. 2:17). He felt both joy and grief as they feel. His body was susceptible to weariness, as yours. His mind, like yours, could be harassed and perplexed. If you have hardships, so had He. . . . Satan could tempt Him. His enemies could annoy Him. . . . Jesus was exposed to hardships, to conflict and temptation, as a man. . . .

"Jesus once stood in age just where you now stand. Your circumstances, your cogitations at this period of your life, Jesus has had. He cannot overlook you at this critical period. He sees your dangers. He is acquainted with your temptations. He invites you to follow His example."

From the same letter 17, 1878, the following is found in *Our High Calling*, p. 59: "Jesus was sinless and had no dread of the consequences of sin. With this exception His condition was as yours."

The Spirit of Prophecy, vol. 3, p. 261: "He who considered it not robbery to be equal with God, once trod the earth, bearing our suffering and sorrowing nature."

1881:

Signs of the Times, June 23, 1881: "Jesus was interested in children. He did not step into our world a fully matured man. Christ was a child; He had the experience of a child; He felt the disappointments and trials that children feel; He knew the temptations of children and youth. But Christ was in His child life and youthful life an example to all children and youth. In childhood His hands were engaged in useful acts. In youth He worked at the carpenter's trade with His father, and was subject to His parents, thus giving in His life a lesson to all children and young. If Christ had never been a child Himself, the youth might now think that He could not sympathize with them." (Note: while the statement is in the original *Signs of the Times* dated June 23, 1881, it did not get copied into the bound volumes.)

1882:

Testimonies for the Church, vol. 5, p. 177: "His [any sinner's] own consent must be first gained; the soul must purpose the sinful act before passion can dominate over reason or iniquity triumph over conscience. Temptation, however strong, is never an excuse for sin. . . . Cry unto the Lord, tempted soul. Cast yourself, helpless, unworthy, upon Jesus, and claim His very promise. The Lord will hear. He knows how strong are the inclinations of the natural heart, and He will help in every time of temptation."

Review and Herald, Feb. 28, 1882: "Not only did Christ die as our sacrifice, but He lived as our example. In His human nature He stands, complete, perfect, spotless. To be a Christian is to be Christlike. Our entire being, soul, body, and spirit, must be purified, ennobled, sanctified, until we shall reflect His image and imitate His example."

1883:

Signs of the Times, Apr. 5, 1883: "The unsullied purity of the childhood, youth, and manhood of Christ, which Satan could not taint, annoyed him exceedingly. . . . And when he found that all his temptations prevailed nothing in moving Christ from the steadfast integrity, or in marring the spotless purity of the youthful Galilean, he was perplexed and enraged. . . .

"Every temptation that seems so afflicting to man in his daily life, so difficult to resist and overcome, was brought to bear upon the Son of God in as much greater degree as his excellence of character was superior to that of fallen man. . . .

"[Satan's] most wily temptations Christ has tested and conquered in behalf of man. It is impossible for man to be tempted above what he is able to bear while he relies upon Jesus, the infinite Conqueror."

1884:

Signs of the Times, Apr. 17, 1884: "Jesus knows our infirmities, and has Himself shared our experience in all things but in sin; therefore He has prepared for us a path suited to our strength and capacity."

Review and Herald, May 27, 1884: "Just before His cruel death, Jesus said, 'The prince of this world cometh, and hath nothing in me.' Satan could find nothing in the Son of God that would enable him to gain a victory. He had kept His Father's commandments; and there was no sin in Him that Satan could triumph over, no weakness or defect that he could use to his advantage. But we are sinful by nature, and we have a work to do to cleanse the soul-temple of every defilement. Let us improve this precious privilege to confess our faults one to another, and pray one for another, that we may be healed."

Review and Herald, Oct. 21, 1884: "Benevolence, gentleness, patience, nobility of thought and action, and the love of God, if cherished permanently, impress the countenance, and win souls, and give power in preaching. If this is possible in fallen man, who is often humbled through a sense of his sinfulness, what power must have attended the ministry of Jesus, who was pure, spotless, and undefiled, though dwelling in a world all seared and marred by the curse."

1885:

Testimonies for the Church, vol. 5, p. 422 (cf. *Questions on Doctrine*, pp. 654, 655): "It was a continual pain to Him to be brought in contact with the enmity, depravity, and impurity which Satan had brought in. . . . 'He . . . suffered being tempted,' suffered in proportion to the perfection of His holiness. But the prince of darkness found nothing in Him; not a single thought or feeling responded to temptation."

Review and Herald, Feb. 10, 1885: "I had freedom and power in presenting Jesus, who took upon Himself the infirmities and bore the grief and sorrows of humanity and conquered in our behalf. He was made like unto His brethren, with the same susceptibilities, mental and physical. He was tempted in all points like as we are, yet without sin; and He knows how to succor those who are tempted. Are you harassed and perplexed? So was Jesus. Do you feel the need of encouragement? So did Jesus. As Satan tempts you, so he tempted the Majesty of heaven."

Review and Herald, May 19, 1885: "He was unsullied with corruption, a stranger to sin; yet He endured agony which required help and support from His Father, and He prayed often with strong crying and tears. He prayed for His disciples and for Himself, thus identifying Himself with the needs, the weaknesses, and the failings which are common to humanity. He was a mighty petitioner, not possessing the passions of our human, fallen natures, but compassed with like infirmities, tempted in all points even as we are."

1886:

Review and Herald, Mar. 9, 1886: "When Christ went into the wilderness of temptation after His baptism, it was to meet the wily foe in conflict. Satan did not at first appear to Christ in his true character, but as a bright, beautiful, attractive angel sent to Him with a message direct from His Father in heaven. This was a temptation to Christ. His humanity made it a temptation to Him. It was only by trusting in His Father that He could resist these temptations. He walked by faith as we must walk by faith. . . . The temptations that He endured were as much more severe than those which come upon us as His character is more exalted than ours."

Review and Herald, Aug. 17, 1886: "He was a mighty petitioner, possessing not the passions of our human, fallen natures, but compassed with like infirmities, tempted in all points even as we are. Jesus endured agony which required help and support from His Father. Christ is our example."

Review and Herald, Sept. 21, 1886 (cf. *Questions on Doctrine*, p. 677): "Justice demanded the sufferings of a man. Christ, equal with God, gave the sufferings of a God. He needed no atonement. . . . The suffering of Christ was in correspondence with His spotless purity; His depth of agony, proportionate to the dignity and grandeur of His character."

Youth's Instructor, Oct. 20, 1886: "He for our sakes laid aside His royal robe, stepped down from the throne in heaven, and condescended to clothe His divinity with humility, and became like one of us except in sin, that His life and character should be a pattern for all to copy, that they might have the precious gift of eternal life."

1887:

Signs of the Times, Aug. 4, 1887: "Man can never know the strength of the temptations to which the Son of God was subjected. All the temptations that seem so afflicting to man in his daily life, so difficult to resist and overcome, were brought to bear upon Him in as much greater degree as He is superior in His excellence of character to fallen man."

Review and Herald, Nov. 8, 1887 (cf. *Questions on Doctrine*, p. 655): "Christ, the sinless One, upon whom the Holy Spirit was bestowed without measure, constantly acknowledged His dependence upon God, and sought fresh supplies from the Source of strength and wisdom. How much more should finite, erring man feel his need of help from God every hour and every moment. . . .

[two paragraphs later] "Would that we could comprehend the significance of the words, 'Christ suffered, being tempted.' While He was free from the taint of sin, the refined sensibilities of His holy nature rendered contact with evil unspeakably painful to Him. Yet with human nature upon Him, He met the arch apostate face to face, and single-handed withstood the foe of His throne. Not even by a thought could Christ be brought to yield to the power of temptation. Satan finds in human hearts some point where he can gain a foot-hold; some sinful desire is cherished, by means of which his temptations assert their power. But Christ declared of Himself, 'The Prince of this world cometh, and hath nothing in me.' The storms of temptation burst upon Him, but they could not cause Him to swerve from His allegiance to God."

Signs of the Times, Nov. 24, 1887: "He passed step by step over the ground that man had trodden, and was 'tempted in all points like as we are, yet without sin.' Where man stumbled and fell, Jesus came off more than conqueror. Had He failed on one point, in reference to the law, all would have been lost; He would not have been a perfect offering, nor could He have satisfied the demands of the law; but He conquered where Adam failed, and by loyalty to God, under the severest trials, became a perfect pattern and example for our imitation, and He is able to succor those who are tempted. There is enough in this idea to fill our hearts with joy and gratitude every day of our lives. He took our nature upon Him that He might become acquainted with our trials and sorrows, and, knowing all our experience, He stands as Mediator and Intercessor before the Father."

1888:

Review and Herald, Mar. 27, 1888: "The Bible presents the law of God as a perfect standard by which to shape the life and character. The only perfect example of obedience to its precepts is found in the Son of

God, the Saviour of lost mankind. There is no stain of unrighteousness upon Him, and we are bidden to follow in His steps."

Review and Herald, July 17, 1888: "When man was lost, the Son of God said, I will redeem him, I will become his surety and substitute. He laid aside His royal robes, clothed His divinity with humanity, stepped down from the royal throne, that He might reach the very depth of human woe and temptation, lift up our fallen natures, and make it possible for us to be overcomers."

Review and Herald, Sept. 11, 1888 (cf. *That I May Know Him*, p. 339): "Christ was not insensible to ignominy and disgrace. He felt it all most bitterly. He felt it as much more deeply and acutely than we can feel suffering, as His nature was more exalted, and pure, and holy than that of the sinful race for whom He suffered."

Review and Herald, Dec. 11, 1888: "He who was one with the Father stepped down from the glorious throne in heaven, . . . and clothed His divinity with humanity, thus bringing Himself to the level of man's feeble faculties. . . . The highest gift that Heaven could bestow was given to ransom fallen humanity."

1889:

Signs of the Times, May 20, 1889: "He came into a world all marred and scarred by the curse. He took upon Him humanity that He might know the infirmities and temptations of humanity, that He might know how to help and save men."

Letter 5, 1889 (cf. *The Ellen G. White 1888 Materials*, vol. 1, p. 332, and *Seventh-day Adventist Bible Commentary*, vol. 7, p. 904): "Christ could have done nothing during His earthly ministry in saving fallen man if the divine had not been blended with the human. The limited capacity of man cannot define this wonderful mystery—the blending of the two natures, the divine and the human. It can never be explained. Man must wonder and be silent. And yet man is privileged to be a partaker of the divine nature, and in this way he can to some degree enter into the mystery."

Signs of the Times, July 29, 1889: "Christ was the ladder that Jacob saw. Christ is the link that binds earth to Heaven, and connects finite man with the infinite God. This ladder reaches from the lowest degradation of earth and humanity to the highest heavens. . . .

[four paragraphs later] "[Christ] came into the world that He might understand all the needs of fallen humanity."

Review and Herald, Oct. 1, 1889: "We cannot explain the great mystery of the plan of redemption. Jesus took upon Himself humanity, that He might reach humanity; but we cannot explain how divinity was clothed with humanity. An angel would not have known how to sympathize with fallen man, but Christ came to the world and suffered all our temptations, and carried all our griefs. Are you not glad that He was tempted in all points like as we are, and yet without sin? Our hearts should be filled with gratitude to Him. We should be able to present to God a continual thank-offering for His wonderful love. Jesus can be touched with the feeling of our infirmities. When we are in sorrow and trouble and temptation, we need not think nobody knows, nobody can understand. O, no; Jesus has passed over every step of the ground before you, and He knows all about it."

Review and Herald, Dec. 24, 1889: "Jesus clothed His divinity with humanity that He might have an experience in all that pertains to human life. He did not leave plans for the welfare of youth and children in obscurity and uncertainty. He became a child, and in His life we find an example of what is the proper development of childhood."

1890:

Manuscript 57, 1890 (cf. *Manuscript Releases,* vol. 16, p. 182): "He had not taken on Him even the nature of angels, but humanity, perfectly identical with our own nature, except without the taint of sin. . . . He had reason, conscience, memory, will, and affections of the human soul which was united with His divine nature.

"Our Lord was tempted as man is tempted. He was capable of yielding to temptations, as are human beings. His finite nature was pure and spotless, but the divine nature . . . was not humanized; neither was humanity deified by the blending or union of the two natures; each retained its essential character and properties.

"But here we must not become in our ideas common and earthly, and in our perverted ideas we must not think that the liability of Christ to yield to Satan's temptations degraded His humanity and He possessed the same sinful, corrupt propensities as man.

"The divine nature, combined with the human, made Him capable of yielding to Satan's temptations. Here the test to Christ was far greater than that of Adam and Eve, for Christ took our nature, *fallen* but not corrupted, and would not be corrupted unless He received the words of Satan in the place of the words of God. To suppose He was not capable of yielding to temptation places Him where He cannot be a perfect example for man, and the force and the power of this part of Christ's humiliation, which is the most eventful, is no instruction or help to human beings. . . .

"He descended in His humiliation to be tempted as man would be tempted, and His nature was that of man, capable of yielding to temptation. His very purity and holiness were assailed by a fallen foe, the very one that became corrupted and then was ejected from heaven. How deeply and keenly must Christ have felt this humiliation.

"How do fallen angels look upon this pure and uncontaminated One, the Prince of life . . ."

Review and Herald, Feb. 18, 1890: "Letters have been coming in to me, affirming that Christ could not have had the same nature as man, for if He had, He would have fallen under similar temptations. If He did not have man's nature, He could not be our example. If He was not a partaker of our nature, He could not have been tempted as man has been. . . . His temptation and victory tell us that humanity must copy the Pattern; man must become a partaker of the divine nature.

"In Christ, divinity and humanity were combined. Divinity was not degraded to humanity; divinity held its place, but humanity by being united to divinity, withstood the fiercest test of temptation in the wilderness. . . . But the plan of God, devised for the salvation of man, provided that Christ should know hunger, and poverty, and every phase of man's experience."

Manuscript 16, 1890 (cf. *Seventh-day Adventist Bible Commentary*, vol. 7, p. 907; *Manuscript Releases*, vol. 17, pp. 336, 337): "In Christ dwelt the fullness of the Godhead bodily. This is why, although He was tempted in all points like as we are, He stood before the world, from His first entrance into it, untainted by corruption, though surrounded by it. Are we not also to become partakers of that fullness, and is it not thus, and thus only, that we can overcome as He overcame?"

"Those who claim that it was not possible for Christ to sin cannot believe that He really took upon Himself human nature; but was not Christ actually tempted, not only by Satan in the wilderness, but all through His life, from childhood to manhood? In all points He was tempted as we are, and because He successfully resisted temptation under every form, He gave man the perfect example, and through the ample provisions Christ has made, we may become partakers of the divine nature."

Manuscript 58, 1890: "He assumed human nature, with its infirmities, its liabilities, its temptations."

1891:

Review and Herald, Apr. 28, 1891: "In His humanity He has become acquainted with all the difficulties that beset humanity."

Signs of the Times, Aug. 24, 1891: "[Jesus] is the 'daysman' between a holy God and our sinful humanity—one who can 'lay His hand on us both.'"

1892:

Manuscript 6, 1892 (cf. Paulson Collection, p. 141): "If we do our best, exercise our entrusted capabilities with the sole purpose of doing our Master's work and promoting His glory, the smallest talent, the humblest service, may become a consecrated gift, made acceptable by the fragrance of His own merit."

Review and Herald, Apr. 1, 1892: "But many say that Jesus was not like us, that He was not as we are in the world, that He was divine, and that we cannot overcome as He overcame. But Paul writes, 'Verily he took not on him the nature of angels; but he took on him the seed of Abraham. Wherefore in all things it behoved him to be made like unto his brethren.'"

Signs of the Times, Nov. 21, 1892 (though this statement was originally published in the *Signs*, Nov. 21, 1892, the statement was actually written on May 29, 1892, as Letter 27; it is also listed in *In Heavenly Places*, p. 155, as taken from undated MS 73. Ellen White later revised it for further publication. We will cite it as found in the *Signs*, Nov 21, 1892): "If you indulge in slang phrases and foolish talk, you bring forth from the treasure of the heart evil things. . . .

[three paragraphs later] "He [Christ] left the glories of heaven, and clothed His divinity with humanity, and subjected Himself to sorrow, and shame, and reproach, abuse, denial, and crucifixion. Though He had all the strength of the passion of humanity, never did He yield to temptation to do that which was not pure and elevating and ennobling."

Review and Herald, July 19, 1892: "Jesus has been over the ground. He knows the power of every temptation. He knows just how to meet every emergency, and how to guide you through every path of danger."

Manuscript 1, 1892 (cf. *Selected Messages*, book 3, pp. 136-141; *Signs of the Times*, Apr. 10, 1893; *Seventh-day Adventist Bible Commentary*, vol. 7, p. 929): "Satan, the fallen angel, had declared that no man could keep the law of God after the disobedience of Adam. . . .

"The Son of God placed Himself in the sinner's stead, and passed over the ground where Adam fell, and endured the temptation in the wilderness, which was a hundredfold stronger than was or ever will be brought to bear upon the human race. Jesus resisted the temptations of Satan in the same manner that every tempted soul may resist, by referring him to the inspired record and saying, 'It is written.'

"Christ overcame the temptations of Satan as a man. Every man may overcome as Christ overcame. . . . He redeemed Adam's disgraceful failure and fall, and was conqueror, thus testifying to all the unfallen worlds and to fallen humanity that man could keep the commandments of God through the divine power granted to him of heaven. Jesus . . . endured temptation for us, overcame in our behalf to show us how we may overcome. . . .

"The world's Redeemer came not only to be a sacrifice for sin but to be an example to man in all things, a holy, human character. . . .

"His practical example left us a plain pattern which we are to copy. . . .

"Not only did Christ give explicit rules showing how we may become obedient children but He showed us in His own life and character just how to do those things which are right and acceptable with God, so there is no excuse why we should not do those things which are pleasing in His sight.

"We are ever to be thankful that Jesus has proved to us by actual facts that man can keep the commandments of God, giving contradiction to Satan's falsehood that man cannot keep them. The Great Teacher came to our world to stand at the head of humanity, to thus elevate and sanctify humanity by His holy obedience to all of God's requirements showing it is possible to obey all the commandments of God. He has demonstrated that a lifelong obedience is possible. Thus He gives chosen, representative men to the world, as the Father gave the Son, to exemplify in their life the life of Jesus Christ.

"We need not place the obedience of Christ by itself as something for which He was particularly adapted, by His particular divine nature, for He stood before God as man's representative and was tempted as man's substitute and surety. If Christ had a special power which it is not the privilege of man to have, Satan would have made capital of this matter. The work of Christ was to take from the claims of Satan his control of man, and He could do this only in the way that He came—a man, tempted as a man, rendering the obedience of a man. . . .

"Bear in mind that Christ's overcoming and obedience is that of a true human being. In our conclusions, we make many mistakes because of our erroneous views of the human nature of our Lord. When we give to His human nature a power that it is not possible for man to have in his conflicts with Satan, we destroy the completeness of His humanity. His imputed grace and power He gives to all who receive Him by faith. The obedience of Christ to His Father was the same obedience that is required of man. . . .

"He came not to our world to give the obedience of a lesser God to a greater, but as a man to obey God's Holy Law, and in this way He is our example. . . .

"The Lord Jesus came to our world, not to reveal what a God could do, but what a man could do, through faith in God's power to help in every emergency. . . .

"Jesus, the world's Redeemer, could only keep the commandments of God in the same way that humanity can keep them."

Bible Echo, Nov. 15, 1892: "The great work of redemption could be carried out by the Redeemer only as He took the place of fallen man. . . . When Adam was assailed by the tempter, none of the effects of sin were upon him, but he was surrounded by the glories of Eden. But it was not thus with Jesus, for, bearing the infirmities of degenerate humanity, He entered the wilderness to cope with the mighty foe, that He might lift man up from the lowest depths of his degradation."

Review and Herald, Dec. 20, 1892: "Hating sin with a perfect hatred, He yet gathered to His soul the sins of the whole world, as He trod the path to Calvary, suffering the penalty of the transgressor. Guiltless, He bore the punishment of the guilty; innocent, yet offering Himself to bear the penalty of the transgression of the law of God. . . . In assuming the nature of man, He placed Himself where He was wounded for our transgressions. . . .

"In His humanity Christ was tried with as much greater temptation, with as much more persevering energy than man is tried by the evil one, as His nature was greater than man's. This is a deep mysterious truth, that Christ is bound to humanity by the most sensitive sympathies. The evil works, the evil thoughts, the evil words of every son and daughter of Adam press upon His divine soul. The sins of men called for retribution upon Himself; for He had become man's substitute, and took upon Him the sins of the world. He bore the sins of every sinner; for all transgressions were imputed unto Him. . . . No man of earth nor angel of heaven could have paid the penalty of sin. Jesus was the only one who could save rebellious man. In Him divinity and humanity were combined, and this was what gave efficiency to the sacrifice made on Calvary's cross."

1893:

Signs of the Times, Feb. 20, 1893: "He humbled Himself to pass through man's experiences. . . . Knowing all the steps in the path of His humiliation, He refused not to descend step by step to the depths of man's woe, that He might make expiation for the sins of the condemned, perishing world. What humility was this! It amazed the angels. . . . Sinless and exalted by nature, the Son of God consented to take the habiliments of humanity, to become one with the fallen race. The eternal Word consented to be made flesh. God became man."

Review and Herald, Mar. 28, 1893: "Christ was free from every taint of selfishness."

Review and Herald, Apr. 25, 1893: "Jesus reached to the very depth of human woe and misery, and His love attracts man to Himself. Through the agency of the Holy Spirit, He lifts the mind up from its degradation, and fastens it upon the eternal reality. Through the merits of Christ man may be able to exercise the noblest powers of his being, and expel sin from his soul."

Manuscript 94, 1893 (cf. *Selected Messages,* book 3, pp. 129-131): "In your letter in regard to the temptations of Christ, you say; 'If He was One with God He could not fall'. . . The point you inquire of me is, In our Lord's great scene of conflict in the wilderness, apparently under the power of Satan and his angels, was He capable, in His human nature, of yielding to these temptations? . . .

"As God He could not be tempted: but as a man He could be tempted, and that strongly, and could yield to the temptations. His human nature must pass through the same test and trial Adam and Eve passed through. His human nature was created; it did not even possess the angelic powers. It was human, identical with our own. He was passing over the ground where Adam fell. He was now where, if He endured the test and trial in behalf of the fallen race, He would redeem Adam's disgraceful failure and fall, in our own humanity.

"A human body and a human mind were His. He was bone of our bone and flesh of our flesh. He was subjected to poverty from His first entrance into the world. He was subject to disappointment and trial in His own home, among His own brethren. . . . He came into our world to maintain a pure, sinless character, and to refute Satan's lie that it was not possible for human beings to keep the law of God. Christ came to live the law in His human character in just that way in which all may live the law in human nature if they will do as Christ was doing. . . .

"Abundant provision has been made that finite, fallen man may so connect with God that, through the same Source by which Christ overcame in His human nature, he may stand firmly against every temptation, as did Christ. . . .

"Through the provision made when God and the Son of God made a covenant to rescue man from the bondage of Satan, every facility was provided that human nature should come into union with His divine nature. . . .

"The Godhead was not made human, and the human was not deified by the blending together of the two natures. Christ did not possess the same sinful, corrupt, fallen disloyalty we possess, for then He could not be a perfect offering."

1894:

Review and Herald, Jan. 23, 1894: "Jesus Christ has given Himself as a complete offering in behalf of every fallen son and daughter of Adam. O, what humiliation He bore! How He descended, step after step, lower and lower in the path of humiliation, yet He never degraded His soul with one foul blot of sin! All that He suffered, that He might lift you up, cleanse, refine, ennoble you, and place you as a joint heir with Himself upon His throne."

Review and Herald, Apr. 24, 1894: "Human weakness, human necessities were upon Him, and he felt keenly the want of food and the results of His long fast."

Youth's Instructor, Aug. 16, 1894 (cf. *That I May Know Him,* p. 288): "No human being has ever possessed so sensitive a nature as did the sinless, holy One of God, who stood as head and representative of what humanity may become through the imparting of the divine nature. To those who believe in Christ as their personal Saviour, He imputes His merit and imparts His power."

Review and Herald, Oct. 23, 1894: "It is by living out the truth in human life that souls are to be reached. As the Son of God in human form was perfect in His life, so He requires that His followers shall be perfect in their lives. He was made in all things like unto His brethren. He hungered, He thirsted, He was weary, He slept, He wept, and yet He was the blameless Son of God, He was God in the flesh. He was tempted in all points like as we are, yet without sin, and we have not a high-priest that cannot be touched with the feeling of our infirmities. He knows how to succor those that are tempted."

1895:

Review and Herald, Feb. 5, 1895: "As Christ humbled Himself, and took upon Himself our nature, He is acquainted with our necessities, and has Himself borne the heaviest temptations that man will have to bear, has conquered the enemy in resisting his suggestions, in order that man may learn how to be conqueror. He was clothed with a body like ours, and in every respect suffered what man will suffer, and very much more. We shall never be called upon to suffer as Christ suffered; for the sins not of one, but the sins of the whole world were laid upon Christ. . . .

"Christ is our pattern, the perfect and holy example that has been given us to follow. We can never equal the pattern; but we may imitate and resemble it according to our ability."

General Conference Bulletin, Feb. 25, 1895: "Jesus assumed humanity that He might treat humanity. He brings men under the transforming power of truth by meeting them where they are. He gains access to the heart by securing sympathy and confidence, making all feel that His identification with their nature and interest is complete."

Review and Herald, Apr. 23, 1895: "Christ's mission was not to explain the complexity of His nature, but to give abundant light to those who would receive it by faith. Fallen men who should believe on Him would receive the full advantage which could be produced through the mysterious union of humanity and divinity."

Signs of the Times, May 16, 1895: "We are too much in the habit of thinking that the Son of God was a being so entirely exalted above us that it is an impossibility for Him to enter into our trials and temptations, and that He can have no sympathy with us in our weakness and frailties. This is because we do not take in the fact of His oneness with humanity."

Review and Herald, June 25, 1895 (cf. *Selected Messages,* book 1, p. 264): "It is a knowledge of Christ as the sin-bearer, as the propitiation for our iniquities, that enables us to live a life of holiness. . . .

"Our Saviour clothed His divinity with humanity. He employed the human faculties, for only by adopting these could He be comprehended by humanity. Only humanity could reach humanity. . . . He blessed the world by living out in human flesh the life of God, thus showing that He had the power to unite humanity to divinity."

Review and Herald, July 9, 1895: "He in whom 'dwelleth all the fullness of the Godhead bodily' descended to our world, humiliated Himself by clothing His divinity with humanity, that through humanity He might reach the human family. While He embraces the human race with His human arm, He grasps the throne of God with His divine arm, thus uniting humanity to divinity. The Majesty of heaven, the King of glory, descended the path of humiliation step by step until He reached the lowest point possible for humanity to experience; and why? That He might be able to reach even the lowest of mankind, sunken in the very depths of degradation though they be, that He might be able to elevate them to the hights (sic) of heaven."

Review and Herald, Oct. 29, 1895: "Satan assailed Christ through every conceivable form of temptation."

Manuscript 21, 1895 (cf. *Seventh-day Adventist Bible Commentary,* vol. 7, p. 925): "He came as a helpless babe, bearing the humanity we bear. . . . Christ clothed His divinity with humanity, that humanity might touch humanity; that He might live with humanity, and bear all the trials and afflictions of man. He was tempted in all points like as we are, yet without sin. In His humanity He understood all the temptations that will come to man."

Youth's Instructor, Nov. 21, 1895 (cf. *That I May Know Him*, p. 26; *Selected Messages*, book 3, pp. 127, 128): "He was to be like those who belonged to the human family and to the Jewish race. His features were to be like those of other human beings, and He was not to have such beauty of person as to make people point Him out as different from others. He was to come as one of the human family, and to stand as a man before heaven and earth. He had come to take man's place, to pledge Himself in man's behalf, to pay the debt that sinners owed. He was to live a pure life on the earth, and show that Satan had told a falsehood when he claimed that the human family belonged to him forever, and that God could not take men out of his hands."

Letter 8, 1895 (sent to W.L.H. Baker in late 1895 or early 1896; Manuscript Release 414; I cite it as found in Ralph Larson, *The Word Was Made Flesh*, pp. 314, 315 [I will cite only the Christological portions; for the entire letter, cf. Larson and compare the citations from this letter in *Questions on Doctrine*, pp. 651 and 652, and *Seventh-day Adventist Bible Commentary*, vol. 5, pp. 1128, 1129]):

"Be careful, exceedingly careful as to how you dwell upon the human nature of Christ. Do not set Him before the people as a man with the propensities of sin. He is the second Adam. The first Adam was created a pure, sinless being, without a taint of sin upon him; he was in the image of God. He could fall, and he did fall through transgressing. Because of sin, his posterity was born with inherent propensities of disobedience. But Jesus Christ was the only begotten Son of God. He took upon Himself human nature, and was tempted in all points as human nature is tempted. He could have sinned; He could have fallen, but not for one moment was there in Him an evil propensity. He was assailed with temptations in the wilderness, as Adam was assailed with temptations in Eden.

"Bro. Baker, avoid every question in relation to the humanity of Christ which is liable to be misunderstood. Truth lies close to the track of presumption. In treating upon the humanity of Christ, you need to guard strenuously every assertion, lest your words be taken to mean more than they imply, and thus you lose or dim the clear perceptions of His humanity as combined with divinity. His birth was a miracle of God; for, said the angel, 'Behold thou shalt conceive in thy womb, and bring forth a son, and shalt call his name Jesus. He shall be great and shall be called the son of the Highest; and the Lord God shall give unto him the throne of his Father David: And he shall reign over the house of Jacob forever; and of his kingdom there shall be no end. Then said Mary unto the angel, How shall this be, seeing that I know not a man? And the angel answered and said unto her, The Holy Ghost shall come upon thee, and the power of the Highest shall overshadow thee; therefore also that holy thing which shall be born of thee shall be called the Son of God.'

"These words are not addressed to any human being, except to the Son of the Infinite God. Never, in any way, leave the slightest impression upon human minds that a taint of or inclination to corruption rested upon Christ, or that He in any way yielded to corruption. He was tempted in all points like as man is tempted, yet He is called that holy thing. It is a mystery that is left unexplained to mortals that Christ could be tempted in all points like as we are, and yet be without sin. The incarnation of Christ has ever been, and will ever remain a mystery. That which is revealed is for us and for our children, but let every human being be warned from the ground of making Christ altogether human, such an one as ourselves: for it cannot be. The exact time when humanity blended with divinity, it is not necessary for us to know. We are to keep our feet on the rock, Christ Jesus, as God revealed in humanity.

"I perceive that there is danger in approaching subjects which dwell on the humanity of the Son of the infinite God. He did humble Himself when He saw He was in fashion as a man, that He might understand the force of all temptations wherewith man is beset.

"The first Adam fell: the second Adam held fast to God and His word under the most trying circumstances, and His faith in His Father's goodness, mercy, and love did not waver for one moment. 'It is written' was His weapon of resistance, and it is the sword of the Spirit which every human being is to use. 'Hereafter I will not talk much with you: for the prince of this world cometh, and hath nothing in me'—nothing to respond to temptation. Not one occasion has been given in response to His manifold temptations. Not once did Christ step on Satan's ground, to give him any advantage. Satan found nothing in Him to encourage his advances."

1896:

Signs of the Times, Jan. 16, 1896: "Christ . . . transgressed not the law of God in any particular. More than this, He removed every excuse from fallen man that he could urge for a reason for not keeping the law of God. Christ was compassed with infirmities of humanity, He was beset with the fiercest temptations, tempted on all points like as men, yet He developed a perfectly upright character. No taint of sin was found upon Him. . . .

"The humanity of Christ is called 'that holy thing.' The inspired record says of Christ, 'He did no sin,' He 'knew no sin,' and 'in him was no sin.'"

Letter 106, 1896 (cf. *Seventh-day Adventist Bible Commentary*, vol. 5, p. 1124): "He was not only made flesh, but He was made in the likeness of sinful flesh."

Signs of the Times, Apr. 9, 1896: "The words of Christ encourage parents to bring their little ones to Jesus. They may be wayward, and possess passions like those of humanity, but this should not deter us from bringing them to Christ. He blessed children that were possessed of passions like His own."

Review and Herald, May 19, 1896: "[Christ] was the Creator of heaven and earth; and yet while upon earth, He became weary, as men do, and sought rest from the continual pressure of labor. He who made the ocean, who controls the waters of the great deep, who opened the springs and channels of the earth, felt it necessary to rest at Jacob's well, and to ask a drink of water from a strange Samaritan woman."

Letter 106, 1896 (cf. *Seventh-day Adventist Bible Commentary*, vol. 5, p. 1124): "It was not a make-believe humanity that Christ took upon Himself. He took human nature and lived human nature. . . . He was compassed with infirmities. . . .

"Just that which you may be, He was in human nature. He took our infirmities. He was not only made flesh, but He was made in the likeness of sinful flesh."

Signs of the Times, July 30, 1896 (cf. *Questions on Doctrine*, pp. 647, 648): "There is a mystery surrounding the birth of Christ that can not and need not be explained. . . .

"In contemplating the incarnation of Christ in humanity, we stand baffled before an unfathomable mystery, that the human mind can not comprehend. . . . Divinity and humanity were mysteriously combined, and man and God became one. It is in this union that we find the hope of our fallen race. Looking upon Christ in humanity, we look upon God, and see in Him the brightness of His glory, the express image of His person. . . .

"He understood the temptations of children; for He bore their sorrows and trials. Firm and steadfast was His purpose to do the right. Tho enticed to evil, He refused to depart in a single instance from the strictest truth and rectitude."

The following citations are from *The Desire of Ages*. Since it came off the press in 1898, some might ask why we place the following citations in 1896. Ralph Larson (105) offers this helpful contextual insight on the completion of *The Desire of Ages*: "During the years 1895 and 1896 Ellen White had been putting the finishing touches on *The Desire of Ages*, which she planned to publish in two volumes. On May 6, 1896, she wrote to her son Edson that the first volume was completed (letter 150, 1896)." Thus what follows is what was written in roughly the first half of *The Desire of Ages*):

The Desire of Ages, p. 49: "It would have been an almost infinite humiliation for the Son of God to take man's nature, even when Adam stood in his innocence in Eden. But Jesus accepted humanity when the race had been weakened by four thousand years of sin. Like every child of Adam He accepted the results of the working of the great law of heredity. What these results were is shown in the history of His earthly ancestors. He came with such a heredity to share our sorrows and temptations, and to give us the example of a sinless life."

The Desire of Ages, pp. 50, 51: "The offerings presented to the Lord were to be without blemish. These offerings represented Christ, and from this it is evident that Jesus Himself was free from physical deformity. He was the 'lamb without blemish and without spot' (1 Peter 1:19). His physical structure was not marred by any defect; His body was strong and healthy. And throughout His lifetime He lived in conformity to nature's laws. Physically as well as spiritually, He was an example of what God designed all humanity to be through obedience to His laws."

The Desire of Ages, p. 71: "The life of Jesus was a life in harmony with God. While He was a child, He thought and spoke as a child; but no trace of sin marred the image of God within Him. Yet He was not exempt from temptation. . . . It was necessary for Him to be constantly on guard in order to preserve His purity."

The Desire of Ages, p. 117 (cf. *Review and Herald*, July 28, 1874, and *The Spirit of Prophecy*, vol. 2, p. 88, from which this statement was obviously drawn): "Satan had pointed to Adam's sin as proof that God's law was unjust, and could not be obeyed. In our humanity, Christ was to redeem Adam's failure. But when Adam was assailed by the tempter, none of the effects of sin were upon him. He stood in the strength of perfect manhood, possessing the full vigor of mind and body. He was surrounded with the glories of Eden, and was in daily communion with heavenly beings. It was not thus with Jesus when He entered the wilderness to cope with Satan. For four thousand years the race had been decreasing in physical strength, in mental power, and in moral worth; and Christ took upon Him the infirmities of degenerate humanity. Only thus could He rescue man from the lowest depths of his degradation.

"Many claim that it was impossible for Christ to be overcome by temptation. Then He could not have been placed in Adam's position; He could not have gained the victory that Adam failed to gain. If we have in any sense a more trying conflict than had Christ, then He would not be able to succor us. But our Saviour took humanity, with all its liabilities. He took the nature of man, with the possibility of yielding to temptation. We have nothing to bear which He has not endured."

The Desire of Ages, pp. 122, 123: "In our own strength it is impossible for us to deny the clamors of our fallen nature. Through this channel Satan will bring temptation upon us. Christ knew that the enemy would come to every human being, to take advantage of hereditary weakness, and by his false insinuations to ensnare all whose trust is not in God. And by passing over the ground which man must travel, our Lord has prepared the way for us to overcome."

The Desire of Ages, p. 123: "There was in Him nothing that responded to Satan's sophistry. He did not consent to sin. Not even by a thought did He yield to temptation. So it may be with us. Christ's humanity was united with divinity; He was fitted for the conflict by the indwelling of the Holy Spirit."

The Desire of Ages, pp. 174, 175: "As the image made in the likeness of the destroying serpents was lifted up for their healing, so One made 'in the likeness of sinful flesh' was to be their Redeemer. Rom. 8:3."

The Desire of Ages, p. 266: "But Jesus, coming to dwell in humanity, receives no pollution. His presence has healing virtue for the sinner."

The Desire of Ages, pp. 311, 312: "Jesus was in all things made like unto His brethren. He became flesh, even as we are. He was hungry and thirsty and weary. He was sustained by food and refreshed by sleep. He shared the lot of man; yet He was the blameless Son of God. He was God in the flesh. His character is to be ours. . . .

"Christ is the ladder that Jacob saw, the base resting on the earth, and the topmost round reaching to the gate of heaven, to the very threshold of glory. If that ladder had failed by a single step of reaching the earth, we should have been lost. But Christ reaches us where we are. He took our nature and overcame, that we through taking His nature might overcome. Made 'in the likeness of sinful flesh' (Rom. 8:3), He lived a sinless life. Now by His divinity He lays hold upon the throne of heaven, while by His humanity He reaches us. He bids us by faith in Him attain to the glory of the character of God. Therefore are we to be perfect, even as our 'Father which is in heaven is perfect.'"

Review and Herald, Sept. 22, 1896: "With His long human arm He encircled humanity, while with His divine arm He grasped the throne of the infinite God. And thus man has strength given him that he may overcome Satan, and triumph in God."

Signs of the Times, Nov. 5, 1896: "Christ assumed human nature, to demonstrate to the fallen world, to Satan and his synagogue, to the universe of heaven, and to the worlds unfallen, that human nature, united to His divine nature, could become entirely obedient to the law of God, that His followers by their love and unity would give evidence that the power of redemption is sufficient to enable man to overcome. And He rejoices to think that His prayer that His followers might be sanctified through the truth will be answered; they will be molded by the transforming influence of His grace into a character after the divine similitude."

Review and Herald, Dec. 15, 1896: "Christ, the second Adam, came to a world polluted and marred, to live a life of perfect obedience. . . .

"Clad in the vestments of humanity, the Son of God came down to the level of those He wished to save. In Him was no guile or sinfulness; He was ever pure and undefiled; yet He took upon Him our sinful nature. Clothing His divinity with humanity, that He might associate with fallen humanity, He sought to regain for man that which, by disobedience, Adam had lost for himself and for the world."

1897:

Letter 69, 1897 (cf. *Selected Messages*, book 3, pp. 135, 136): "The great teacher came into our world, not only to atone for sin but to be a teacher both by precept and example. He came to show man how to keep the law in humanity, so that man might have no excuse for following his own defective judgment. We see Christ's obedience. His life was without sin. His lifelong obedience is a reproach to disobedient humanity. The obedience of Christ is not to be put aside as altogether different from the obedience He requires of us individually. Christ has shown us that it is possible for all humanity to obey the laws of God. . . .

[two paragraphs later] "Our Saviour took up the true relationship of a human being as the Son of God. We are sons and daughters of God. In order to know how to behave ourselves circumspectly, we must follow where Christ leads the way. For thirty years He lived the life of a perfect man, meeting the highest standard of perfection. Then let man, however imperfect, hope in God, saying not, 'If I were of a different disposition I would serve God,' but bring himself to Him in true service."

Signs of the Times, Mar. 4, 1897: "With His divinity veiled by humanity, He lived a life of perfect obedience to the law of God."

Signs of the Times, Apr. 22, 1897: "He was subject to the frailties of humanity."

Signs of the Times, June 17, 1897: "He took human nature. He became flesh even as we are. He was oft hungry, thirsty, and weary. He was sustained by food and refreshed by sleep. He had natural affection. . . . While in this world, Christ lived a life of complete humanity in order that He might stand as a representative of the human family. He was tempted in all points like as we are, that He might be able to succor them that are tempted. . . . Passing over the ground where Adam fell, He endured every test that Adam failed to endure. Every temptation that could be brought against fallen humanity, He met and overcame.

"Had He not been fully human, Christ could not have been our substitute. . . . But while bearing human nature, He was dependent upon the Omnipotent for His life. In His humanity, He laid hold of the divinity of God; and this every member of the human family has the privilege of doing. Christ did nothing that human nature may not do if it partakes of the divine nature. . . .

[five paragraphs later] "If we repent of our transgression, and receive Christ as the Life-giver, our personal Saviour, we become one with Him, and our will is brought into harmony with the divine will. We become partakers of the life of Christ, which is eternal. We derive immortality from God by receiving the life of Christ; for in Christ dwells all the fullness of the Godhead bodily. This life is the mystical union and cooperation of the divine with the human.

"As children of the first Adam, we partake of the dying nature of Adam."

Signs of the Times, July 22, 1897: "He would clothe Himself in the garb of humanity, and live the life of man from the very beginning. . . .
"Christ assumed humanity, with all its humiliation and service."

Youth's Instructor, Aug. 5, 1897: "Words cannot express the greatness of the love of God for man; but Christ has revealed it in His life in humanity. Only by Himself assuming human nature, and reaching down to the very depths of human misery, could He lift the race from its darkness and despair."

Signs of the Times, Nov. 25, 1897: "The time had come for Satan's last attempt [referring to Gethsemane and Calvary] to overcome Christ. But Christ declared, He hath nothing in me, no sin that brings me in his power. He can find nothing in me that responds to his satanic suggestions. No other being could say this but the One who was offering up His life as a sinless sacrifice for a sinful race."

Manuscript 143, 1897 (cf. *Manuscript Releases*, vol. 16, pp. 115-117): "Christ . . . took our nature in its deteriorated condition. . . .
"By taking upon Himself man's nature in its fallen condition, . . . He was subject to the infirmities and weaknesses of the flesh with which humanity is encompassed. . . .
"There should not be the faintest misgivings in regard to the perfect freedom from sinfulness in the human nature of Christ."

Signs of the Times, Dec. 9, 1897 (cf. *Seventh-day Adventist Bible Commentary*, vol. 5, p. 1104): "The human nature of Christ was like unto ours, and suffering was more keenly felt by Him; for His spiritual nature was free from every taint of sin. Therefore His desire for the removal of suffering was stronger than human beings can experience. . . .
[two paragraphs later] "The Son of God endured the wrath of God against sin. All the accumulated sin of the world was laid upon the Sin-bearer. . . . He was one with God. Not a taint of corruption was upon Him."

1898:

Signs of the Times, Jan. 20, 1898 (cf. *Seventh-day Adventist Bible Commentary,* vol. 7, p. 904): "He [Christ] suffered in the place of sinful men, taking them into union with Himself. This is the mystery into which angels desire to look."

The Desire of Ages, p. 671: "The power of evil had been strengthening for centuries, and the submission of men to this satanic captivity was amazing."

The Desire of Ages, p. 700: "He suffered in proportion to the perfection of His holiness and His hatred of sin. . . . To be surrounded by human beings under the control of Satan was revolting to Him."

Manuscript 18, 1898 (cf. *That I May Know Him,* p. 67): "In coming to the world in human form, in becoming subject to the law, in revealing to men that He bore their sickness, their sorrow, their guilt, Christ did not become a sinner. He was pure and uncontaminated by any disease. Not one stain of sin was found upon Him. . . . He who was in the health of perfect manhood was as one afflicted with them."

Manuscript 44, 1898 (cf. *Seventh-day Adventist Bible Commentary,* vol. 7, p. 907): "We are not to praise the gospel, but praise Christ. We are not to worship the gospel, but the Lord of gospel. Christ is a perfect representation of God on the one hand, and a perfect specimen of sinless humanity on the other hand. Thus He has combined divinity and humanity."

Youth's Instructor, June 2, 1898: (*Questions on Doctrine,* p. 650): "Christ is called the second Adam. In purity and holiness, connected with God and beloved by God, He began where the first Adam began. Willingly He passed over the ground where Adam fell, and redeemed Adam's failure.

"But the first Adam was in every way more favorably situated than was Christ. . . .

"He, the Commander of all heaven, one with God, clothed His divinity with humanity. He humbled Himself, taking up His abode on the earth, that He might become acquainted with the temptations and trials wherewith man is beset. Before the heavenly universe He unfolded to men the great salvation that His righteousness would bring to all who accept it—an inheritance among the saints and angels in the presence of God.

"Christ was tempted by Satan in a hundredfold severer manner than was Adam, and under circumstances in every way more trying. The deceiver presented himself as an angel of light, but Christ withstood his temptations. He redeemed Adam's disgraceful fall, and saved the world.

"With His human arm, Christ encircled the race, while with His divine arm, He grasped the throne of the Infinite, uniting finite man with the infinite God. He bridged the gulf that sin had made, and connected earth with heaven. In His human nature He maintained the purity of His divine character."

Signs of the Times, June 9, 1898 (this reference was published in *Signs of the Times*, June 9, 1898, but not copied into the bound volumes; cf. *Selected Messages*, book 1, pp. 253-256; *Seventh-day Adventist Bible Commentary*, vol. 5, p. 1131; and *Questions on Doctrine*, p. 651):

"Christ, who knew not the least taint of sin or defilement, took our nature in its deteriorated condition. This was humiliation greater than finite man can comprehend. . . .

"Christ came to the earth, taking humanity and standing as man's representative, to show in the controversy with Satan that man, as God created him, connected with the Father and the Son, could obey every divine requirement. . . .

"'All these things will I give thee, if thou wilt fall down and worship me' (Matt. 4:8, 9). But Christ was unmoved. He felt the strength of this temptation; but He met it in our behalf, and conquered. And He used only the weapons justifiable for human beings to use—the word of Him who is mighty in counsel—'It is written' (Matt. 4:4, 10).

"With what intense interest was this controversy watched by the heavenly angels and the unfallen worlds, as the honor of the law was being vindicated. Not merely for this world, but for the universe of heaven, was the controversy to be forever settled. . . .

"Christ's humanity would demonstrate for eternal ages the question which settled the controversy.

"In taking upon Himself man's nature in its fallen condition, Christ did not in the least participate in its sin. He was subject to the infirmities and weaknesses by which man is encompassed. . . . Could Satan in the least particular have tempted Christ to sin, he would have bruised the Saviour's head. As it was, he could only touch His heel. Had the head of Christ been touched, the hope of the human race would have perished. Divine wrath would have come upon Christ as it came upon Adam. . . .

"We should have no misgivings in regard to the perfect sinlessness of the human nature of Christ. Our faith must be an intelligent faith, looking unto Jesus in perfect confidence, in full and entire faith in the atoning Sacrifice. This is essential that the soul may not be enshrouded in darkness. This holy Substitute is able to save to the uttermost; for He presented to the wondering universe perfect and complete humility in His human character, and perfect obedience to all the requirements of God."

Signs of the Times, June 16, 1898: "His sensibilities were most acute; for in Him was all that is elevated in mind, exalted in sentiment, and fine and delicate in feeling. In His nature was seen the perfection of humanity."

Youth's Instructor, Aug. 4, 1898 (found in *Questions on Doctrine*, p. 656; *Sons and Daughters of God*, p. 48): "He could endure, because He was without one taint of disloyalty or sin."

Youth's Instructor, Sept. 8, 1898: "It is not correct to say, as many writers have said, that Christ was like all children. He was not like all children. Many children are misguided and mismanaged. But Joseph, and especially Mary, kept before them the remembrance of their child's divine Fatherhood. Jesus was instructed in accordance with the sacred character of His mission. His inclination to right was a constant gratification to His parents. . . .

"No one, looking upon the childlike countenance, shining with animation, could say that Christ was just like other children. He was God in human flesh. When urged by His companions to do wrong, divinity flashed through humanity, and He refused decidedly. . . . It was this keen discrimination between right and wrong that often provoked Christ's brothers to anger."

Youth's Instructor, Oct. 13, 1898 (cf. *Selected Messages*, book 1, pp.

244, 245; *Questions on Doctrine*, p. 647): "The humanity of the Son of God is everything to us. It is the golden chain that binds our souls to Christ, and through Christ to God. This is to be our study. Christ was a real man; He gave proof of His humility in becoming a man. Yet He was God in the flesh. When we approach this subject, we would do well to heed the words spoken by Christ to Moses at the burning bush, 'Put off thy shoes from off thy feet, for the place whereon thou standest is holy ground.' We should come to this study with the humility of a learner, with a contrite heart. And the study of the incarnation of Christ is a fruitful field, which will repay the searcher who digs deep for hidden truth. . . .

"The character of Christ on earth revealed divinity, and the gospel which He has given is to be the study of His human heritage."

Letter 97, 1898 (cf. *Manuscript Releases*, vol. 10, p. 173; *Seventh-day Adventist Bible Commentary*, vol. 7, p. 925; *Questions on Doctrine*, p. 666): "As the sin-bearer and priest and representative of man before God, He entered into the life of humanity, bearing our flesh and blood. . . . Christ made a full atonement, giving His life as a ransom for us. He was born without a taint of sin, but came into the world in like manner as the human family. He did not have a mere semblance of a body, but He took human nature, participating in the life of humanity."

Manuscript 166, 1898 (cf. *Manuscript Releases*, vol. 17, p. 26): "To save fallen humanity, the Son of God took humanity upon Him. . . . He consented to an actual union with man. . . .

"Christ did in reality unite the offending nature of man with His own sinless nature, because by this act of condescension, He would be enabled to pour out His blood in behalf of the fallen race."

Youth's Instructor, Dec. 29, 1898 (cf. *Selected Messages*, book 3, p. 133; *Sons and Daughters of God*, p. 25): "He never bore disease in His own flesh; but He carried the sickness of others. When suffering humanity pressed about Him, He who was in the health of perfect manhood was as one afflicted with them. . . .

[eight paragraphs later] "In His life on earth, Christ developed a perfect character, He rendered perfect obedience to His Father's commandments. In coming to the world in human form, in becoming subject to the law, in revealing to men that He bore their sickness, their sorrow, their guilt, He did not become a sinner. Before the Pharisees He could say, 'Which of you convinceth me of sin?' Not one stain of sin was found upon Him. He stood before the world the spotless Lamb of God."

1899:

Letter 32, 1899 (cf. *Seventh-day Adventist Bible Commentary*, vol. 5, p. 1130): "When Jesus took human nature, and became in fashion as a man, He possessed all the human organism. His necessities were the necessities of a man. He had bodily wants to be supplied, bodily weariness to be relieved. By prayer to the Father He was braced for duty and for trial."

Manuscript 19, 1899 (cf. *Welfare Ministry*, p. 287): "Not one impure word escaped His lips. Never did He do a wrong action, for He was the Son of God. Although He possessed a human form, yet He was without a taint of sin."

Signs of the Times, May 10, 1899: "How did the Father answer Christ's prayer?

"For a period of time Christ was on probation. He took humanity on Himself, to stand the test and trial which the first Adam failed to endure. Had He failed in His test and trial, He would have been disobedient to the voice of God, and the world would have been lost.

"Satan has asserted that men could not keep the commandments of God. To prove that they could, Christ became a man, and lived a life of perfect obedience, an evidence to sinful human beings, to the worlds unfallen, and to the heavenly angels, that man could keep God's law through the divine power that is abundantly provided for all that believe. In order to reveal God to the world, to demonstrate as true that which Satan has denied, Christ volunteered to take humanity, and in His power, humanity can obey God. . . .

"He was, as we are, subject to the enemy's temptations. Satan exulted when Christ became a human being, and he compassed His path with every conceivable temptation. Human weakness and tears were His portion; but

He sought unto God, praying with His whole soul, with strong crying and tears; and He was heard in that He feared. The subtlety of the enemy could not ensnare Him while He made God His trust, and was obedient to His words. 'The prince of this world cometh,' He said, 'and hath nothing in me.' He can find nothing in Me which responds to his sophistry.

"Amid impurity, Christ maintained His purity. Satan could not stain or corrupt it. His character revealed a perfect hatred for sin. It was His holiness that stirred against Him all the passion of a profligate world; for by His perfect life He threw upon the world a perpetual reproach, and made manifest the contrast between transgression and the pure, spotless righteousness of One that knew no sin. . . .

"Christ was buffeted with temptations, and convulsed with agony."

Letter 116, 1899 (cf. *Selected Messages*, book 1, p. 95): "These were real temptations, no pretense. Christ 'suffered being tempted' (Heb. 2:18). . . .

[three paragraphs later] "The Son of God in His humanity wrestled with the very same fierce, apparently overwhelming temptations that assail men—temptations to indulgence of appetite, . . ."

Signs of the Times, Dec. 20, 1899 (cf. Manuscript 48, 1899; *Our High Calling*, p. 107): "In His humanity He had the same free will that Adam had in Eden."

Manuscript 165, 1899 (cf. *Questions on Doctrine*, pp. 665, 668, 680; *Manuscript Releases*, vol. 5, p. 114): "Christ declared, where stands Satan's throne, there shall stand My cross, the instrument of humiliation and suffering. No single principle of human nature will I violate. Clothing My divinity with humanity, I will endure every temptation wherewith man is beset. I will call to My aid the powers of heaven, that men and women, imbued with My Spirit, may overcome as I overcame. . . . The working out of My purposes in behalf of degraded humanity requires that divine and human forces be combined. This will be necessary in order to successfully resist the power that would eclipse every ray of light from heaven. . . .

"Christ came to this earth to show that in humanity He could keep the holy law of God. 'I have kept my Father's commandments,' He declared. The Saviour proposed to reestablish the principles of human dependence upon God and cooperation between God and man. . . .

"Christ's identity with man will ever be the power of His influence. He became bone of our bone and flesh of our flesh. . . . He might have cut Himself loose from fallen beings. He might have treated them as sinners deserve to be treated. But instead, He came still nearer to them. He clothed His divine nature with the garb of humanity and demonstrated before the heavenly universe, before the unfallen worlds, and before the fallen world how much God loves the human race. . . .

[one paragraph later] "He stands before the congregation of His redeemed as their sin-burdened, sin-stained surety, but it is their sins He is bearing. All through His life of humiliation and suffering, from the time that He was born an infant in Bethlehem till He hung on the cross of Calvary, and cried in a voice that shook the universe, 'It is finished,' the Saviour was pure and spotless."

1900:

Letter 5, 1900 (cf. *Seventh-day Adventist Bible Commentary*, vol. 7, p. 926): "He became subject to temptation, endangering as it were, His divine attributes."

Manuscript 21, 1900 (cf. *Manuscript Releases*, vol. 17, p. 27): "In all the afflictions of humanity He was afflicted."

Manuscript 50, 1900 (cf. *Selected Messages*, book 1, p. 344): "The religious services, the prayers, the praise, the penitent confession of sin ascend from true believers as incense to the heavenly sanctuary, but passing through the corrupt channels of humanity, they are so defiled that unless purified by blood, they can never be of value with God. They ascend not in spotless purity, and unless the Intercessor, who is at God's right hand, presents and purifies all by His righteousness, it is not acceptable to God. All incense from earthly tabernacles must be moist with the cleansing drops of the blood of Christ. He holds before the Father the censer of His own merits, in which there is no taint of earthly corruption. He gathers into this censer the prayers, the praise, and the confessions of

His people, and with these He puts His own spotless righteousness. Then, perfumed with the merits of Christ's propitiation, the incense comes up before God wholly and entirely acceptable. Then gracious answers are returned.

"Oh, that all may see that everything in obedience, in penitence, in praise and thanksgiving, must be placed upon the glowing fire of the righteousness of Christ. The fragrance of this righteousness ascends like a cloud around the mercy seat."

Manuscript 53, 1900 (cf. *Manuscript Releases*, vol. 17, p. 27): "Christ became one with the human family. . . . Thus He assured them of His complete identification with humanity."

Bible Echo, May 21, 1900 (cf. *Signs of the Times*, July 17, 1900): "He clothed His divinity with humanity, that He might bear all the infirmities and endure all the temptations of humanity."

Review and Herald, June 12, 1900: "Our Redeemer humbled Himself, fully identifying His interests with the interests of humanity. . . . Christ's divinity was so completely veiled that it was difficult for even His disciples to believe in Him; and when He died on the cross, they felt that their hope had perished."

Review and Herald, July 17, 1900: "To save fallen humanity the Son of God took humanity upon Himself. . . . One with God, He alone was capable of accomplishing the work of redemption, and He consented to an actual union with man. In His sinlessness, He would bear every transgression. . . .

"It is a mystery too deep for the human mind to fathom. Christ did in reality unite the offending nature of man with His own sinless nature, because by this act of condescension He would be enabled to pour out His blessings in behalf of the fallen race. Thus He has made it possible for us to partake of His nature. . . . He placed Himself in man's position, becoming capable of suffering. The whole of His earthly life was a preparation for the altar."

Review and Herald, Sept. 25, 1900: "The more humble are our views of ourselves, the more clearly we shall see the spotless character of Jesus. . . . Not to see the marked contrast between Christ and ourselves is not to know ourselves. He who does not abhor himself can not understand the meaning of redemption. To be redeemed means to cease from sin."

Review and Herald, Oct. 2, 1900: "In His human nature He felt the need of the ministration of heavenly angels. He felt the need of His Father's help, as no other human being has ever felt it. . . . As our substitute and surety, He felt every pang of anguish that we can ever feel. He Himself suffered, being tempted."

Signs of the Times, Oct. 17, 1900: "Jesus came to the world as a human being that He might become acquainted with human beings. . . .

"Adam was tempted by the enemy, and he fell. It was not indwelling sin that caused him to yield; for God made him pure and upright, in His own image. He was as faultless as the angels before the throne. There were in him no corrupt principles, no tendencies to evil. But when Christ came to meet the temptations of Satan, He bore the 'likeness of sinful flesh.'"

Youth's Instructor, Dec. 20, 1900 (cf. *Seventh-day Adventist Bible Commentary*, vol. 4, p. 1147): "He took upon Himself fallen, suffering human nature, degraded and defiled by sin. . . . He endured all the temptations wherewith man is beset."

1901:

Manuscript 141, 1901 (cf. *Manuscript Releases*, vol. 17, p. 338; *Seventh-day Adventist Bible Commentary*, vol. 7, p. 926): "The nature of God, whose law had been transgressed, and the nature of Adam, the transgressor, meet in Jesus—the Son of God, and the Son of man."

Manuscript 141, 1901 (cf. *Manuscript Releases*, vol. 17, pp. 336, 337; *Seventh-day Adventist Bible Commentary*, vol. 7, p. 929): "Those who claim that it was not possible for Christ to sin cannot believe that He really took upon Himself human nature. But was not Christ actually tempted, not only by Satan in the wilderness, but all through His life, from childhood to manhood? In all points He was tempted as we are, and because He successfully resisted temptation under every form, He gave man the perfect example, and through the ample provision Christ has made, we may become partakers of the divine nature. . . .

[two paragraphs later] "Jesus was free from all sin and error; there was not a trace of imperfection in His life or character. He maintained spotless purity under circumstances the most trying. . . . Jesus speaks of Himself as well as the Father as God, and claims for Himself perfect righteousness."

Letter 19, 1901 (cf. *Manuscript Releases*, vol. 21, p. 271): "To keep His glory veiled as the child of a fallen race, this was the most severe discipline, to which the Prince of Life could subject Himself."

General Conference Bulletin, Apr. 23, 1901 (cf. *Selected Messages*, book 3, pp. 128, 129): "Laying aside His royal crown, He condescended to step down, step by step, to the level of fallen humanity. . . .

[four paragraphs later] "Christ was suffering as the members of the human family under temptation; but it was not the will of God that He should exercise His divine power in His own behalf. Had He not stood as our representative, Christ's innocence would have exempted Him from all this anguish, but it was because of His innocence that He felt so keenly the assaults of Satan."

Youth's Instructor, Apr. 25, 1901 (cf. *Questions on Doctrine*, pp. 651-654): "Entire justice was done in the atonement. In the place of the sinner, the spotless Son of God received the penalty, and the sinner goes free as long as he receives and holds Christ as his personal Saviour. Though guilty, he is looked upon as innocent. Christ fulfilled every requirement demanded by justice. . . .

"When Christ bowed His head and died, He bore the pillars of Satan's kingdom with Him to the earth. He vanquished Satan in the same nature over which in Eden Satan obtained the victory. The enemy was overcome by Christ in His human nature. The power of the Saviour's Godhead was hidden. He overcame in human nature, relying upon God for power."

Signs of the Times, May 29, 1901 (cf. *Seventh-day Adventist Bible Commentary*, vol. 7, p. 912): "In the fullness of time He was to be revealed in human form. He was to take His position at the head of humanity by taking the nature but not the sinfulness of man."

1902:

Letter 67, 1902 (cf. *Medical Ministry*, p. 181): "He took upon His sinless nature our sinful nature, that He might know how to succor those that are tempted."

Signs of the Times, July 30, 1902: "Clad in the vestments of humanity, the Son of God came down to the level of those He wished to save. In Him was no guile or sinfulness; He was ever pure and undefiled; yet He took upon Him our sinful nature. Clothing His divinity with humanity, that He might associate with fallen humanity, He sought to regain for man that which by disobedience Adam had lost."

Signs of the Times, Dec. 3, 1902: "Christ came to this world as a man, to prove to angels and to men that man may overcome, that in every emergency he may know that the powers of Heaven are ready to help him. Our Saviour took the nature of man with all its possibilities. . . .

[four paragraphs later] "In the wilderness Christ and Satan met in combat, Christ in the weakness of humanity. . . .

[two paragraphs later] "Adam had the advantage over Christ, in that when he was assailed by the tempter, none of the effects of sin were upon Him. . . . It was not thus with Jesus when He entered the wilderness to cope with Satan. For four thousand years the race had been decreasing in physical strength, in mental power, in moral worth; and Christ took upon Him the infirmities of degenerate humanity. Only thus could He rescue man from the lowest depths of degradation."

1903:

Education, p. 78: "Christ alone had experience in all the sorrows and temptations that befall human beings. Never another of woman born was so fiercely beset by temptation; never another bore so heavy a burden of the world's sin and pain. Never was there another whose sympathies were so broad or so tender. A sharer in all the experiences of humanity,

He could feel not only for, but with, every burdened and tempted and struggling one."

Letter 303, 1903 (to Dr. J. H. Kellogg): "Coming, as He did, as a man (to meet and be subjected to) with all the evil tendencies to which man is heir, (working in every conceivable manner to destroy his faith) He made it possible for Himself to be buffeted by human agencies inspired by Satan, the rebel who had been expelled from heaven." (The items in parentheses were written between the lines of the typed text of the letter in Ellen White's own handwriting; for further background on this recently discovered letter, see Appendix C.)

Letter 264, 1903 (cf. *Sons and Daughters of God*, p. 230): "Our Saviour came to this world to endure in human nature all the temptations wherewith man is beset."

1904:

Letter 280, 1904 (cf. *Seventh-day Adventist Bible Commentary*, vol. 5, p. 1113): "Was the human nature of the Son of Mary changed into the divine nature of the Son of God? No; the two natures were mysteriously blended in one person—the man Christ Jesus."

1906:

Review and Herald, Apr. 5, 1906: "Christ did not make believe take human nature; He did verily take it. He did in reality possess human nature."

The Recently Discovered Kellogg Letter of 1903

W hat follows is an explanatory note from William Fagal, director of the White Estate Branch Office in Berrien Springs, Michigan. It was released on January 27, 1994.

Revised Notice
Regarding Kellogg Letter

This letter was found recently in the document files at the Ellen G. White Estate in Silver Spring. At the time of its original typing in 1903 it was given a reference number, as was done with Ellen White's letters, but evidently it never was actually entered into her letter file, because another letter in that file bears the same number. This may account for the fact that it has been overlooked for so long: anyone finding the letter in the document file would assume it was also in the letter file. Only when a White Estate staff member actually cross-checked recently was the discovery made that it was not included in the letter file.

The statement that has attracted the most interest is on page 5, just below the middle of the page. The typewritten sentence reads "Coming, as He [Jesus] did, as a man, *with all the evil tendencies to which man is heir,* He made it possible for Himself to be buffeted by human agencies inspired by Satan, the rebel who had been expelled from heaven" (italics mine). In my own first reading I felt that here finally was a statement in which Ellen White unambiguously ascribed all of the characteristics of "fallen human nature" to Jesus (without, of course, saying that He ever committed sin). Since this matter has been the subject of substantial controversy in the church, I felt we now had a basis for resolving the controversy. But I had not paid attention to Ellen White's own handwritten additions. Just before the phrase in question, a caret ($\wedge$) indicates that the words written above were to be inserted. The statement then would read "Coming, as He did, as a man, *to meet and be subjected to with* [Fagal edited out "with"] *all the evil tendencies to which man is heir,* He made it possible for Himself to be buffeted by human agencies inspired by Satan, the rebel who had been expelled from heaven" (italics mine). (Another handwritten addition, "working in every conceivable manner to destroy his faith," also needs to go into this sentence. By its position it appears to go after "heir.") Unlike my first reading, this reading is open to the interpretation that the evil tendencies are *external* to Christ in the Satan-inspired people who will oppose, buffet, and oppress Him. Though many will still read the statement in harmony with my first reading, others will come to the alternative interpretation. I now think that this statement will not resolve the controversy in the church.

Arrangements are being made to publish at least the portions of the letter that relate to this discussion, and the White Estate is preparing a document that will include the whole letter, in its original form and in an easier-to-read new typing, along with other information about it. [These documents are now available from the White Estate.]

Bibliography

BIBLIOGRAPHY

I. Ellen White Material

The Bible Echo. The Ellen White articles are located in the *Ellen G. White Periodical Resources Collection*, vol. 1. Boise, Idaho: Pacific Press Pub. Assn., 1990.

Child Guidance. Nashville: Southern Pub. Assn., 1954.

Christian Service. Washington, D.C.: General Conference of Seventh-day Adventists, 1946.

Christ's Object Lessons. Washington, D.C.: Review and Herald Pub. Assn., 1941.

Counsels on Sabbath School Work. Washington, D.C.: Review and Herald Pub. Assn., 1938.

Counsels to Parents, Teachers, and Students. Mountain View, Calif.: Pacific Press Pub. Assn., 1943.

Counsels to Writers and Editors. Nashville: Southern Pub. Assn., 1946.

The Desire of Ages. Mountain View, Calif.: Pacific Press Pub. Assn., 1898.

Early Writings. Washington, D.C.: Review and Herald Pub. Assn., 1945.

Education. Mountain View, Calif.: Pacific Press Pub. Assn., 1952.

The Ellen G. White 1888 Material (facsimile reproductions). Washington, D.C.: The Ellen G. White Estate, 1987. 4 vols.

Evangelism. Washington, D.C.: Review and Herald Pub. Assn., 1946.

Faith and Works. Nashville: Southern Pub. Assn., 1979.

General Conference Bulletin, 1895, 1901. The Ellen White articles are located in the *Ellen G. White Periodical Resources Collection*, vol. 1. Boise, Idaho: Pacific Press Pub. Assn., 1990.

The Great Controversy. Mountain View, Calif.: Pacific Press Pub. Assn., 1911.

Historical Sketches of the Foreign Missions of the Seventh-day Adventists. Basel, Switzerland: Imprimerie Polyglotte, 1886.

In Heavenly Places. Washington, D.C.: Review and Herald Pub. Assn., 1967.

Manuscript Releases From the Files of the Letters and the Manuscripts Written by Ellen G. White. Silver Spring, Md.: Ellen G. White Estate, 1990. 21 vols.

Medical Ministry. Mountain View, Calif.: Pacific Press Pub. Assn., 1963.

Our High Calling. Washington, D.C.: Review and Herald Pub. Assn., 1961.

Patriarchs and Prophets. Mountain View, Calif.: Pacific Press Pub. Assn., 1890.

Paulson Collection. Payson, Ariz.: Leaves-of-Autumn, n.d.

Review and Herald Articles (facsimile reprint). Washington, D.C.: Review and Herald Pub. Assn., 1962. 6 vols.

Selected Messages. Washington, D.C.: Review and Herald Pub. Assn., 1958; 1980. 3 books.

Seventh-day Adventist Bible Commentary. Ellen G. White Comments. Washington, D.C.: Review and Herald Pub. Assn., 1952-1957. 7 vols. (Volume 7-A contains, in one convenient setting, all of the Ellen White comments that come at the end of each of the seven volumes of commentary. It also contains the Ellen White collection of primary references from the three appendixes of *Seventh-day Adventists Answer Questions on Doctrine*.)

Seventh-day Adventists Answer Questions on Doctrine. Washington, D.C.: Review and Herald Pub. Assn., 1957. (Appendixes A, B, and C contain an important collection of primary references from Ellen White's published and unpublished writings).

Signs of the Times Articles (facsimile reproduction). Mountain View, Calif.: Pacific Press Pub. Assn., 1974. 4 vols.

Sons and Daughters of God. Washington, D.C.: Review and Herald Pub. Assn., 1955.

The Spirit of Prophecy (facsimile reproduction). Washington, D.C.: Review and Herald Pub. Assn., 1969.

Spiritual Gifts (facsimile reprint). Washington, D.C.: Review and Herald Pub. Assn., 1945. 4 vols.

Steps to Christ. Washington, D.C.: Review and Herald Pub. Assn., 1977.

Testimonies for the Church. Mountain View, Calif.: Pacific Press Pub. Assn., 1948. 9 vols.

That I May Know Him. Washington, D.C.: Review and Herald Pub. Assn., 1964.

Thoughts From the Mount of Blessing. Washington, D.C.: Review and Herald Pub. Assn., 1955.

Welfare Ministry. Washington, D.C.: Review and Herald Pub. Assn., 1952.

Youth's Instructor Articles (facsimile reproduction). Washington, D.C.: Review and Herald Pub. Assn., 1986.

Note: The Ellen White writings feature numerous unpublished manuscripts and letters. Many of these have been printed in different publications, as have many of the periodical articles. Any manuscript, periodical article, or letter that does not have a published reference is on file at the Ellen G. White Estate in Silver Spring, Maryland.

Other Sources

Bibliography

BIBLIOGRAPHY

II. Other Sources

Adams, Roy. *The Sanctuary Doctrine: Three Approaches in the Seventh-day Adventist Church*. Berrien Springs, Mich.: Andrews University Press, 1981.

Dayton, Donald W., and Robert K. Johnston, eds. *The Variety of American Evangelicalism*. Knoxville, Tenn.: University of Tennessee Press, 1991.

Fernandez, Gil G. "Ellen G. White: The Doctrine of the Person of Christ." Ph.D. dissertation, Drew University, 1978.

Graybill, Ronald, Warren Johns, and Tim Poirier. *Henry Melvill and Ellen G. White: A Study of Literary and Theological Relationships*. Washington, D.C.: Ellen G. White Estate, 1982.

Heise, Lyell Vernon. "The Christology of Ellen G. White Letter 8, 1895: an Historical, Contextual, and Analytical Study." Research paper, Andrews University, 1975. Typescript. James White Library, Heritage Room.

Heppenstall, Edward. *The Man Who Is God*. Washington, D.C.: Review and Herald Pub. Assn., 1977.

Knight, George. *From 1888 to Apostasy: The Case of A. T. Jones*. Hagerstown, Md.: Review and Herald Pub. Assn., 1987.

Larson, Ralph. *The Word Was Made Flesh: One Hundred Years of Seventh-day Adventist Christology, 1852-1952*. Cherry Valley, Calif.: Cherrystone Press, 1986.

Melvill, Henry. *Melvill's Sermons*. 3rd ed. New York: 1844.

Moore, A. Leroy. *Adventism in Conflict*. Hagerstown, Md.: Review and Herald Pub. Assn., 1995.

_____ . *The Theology Crisis*. Corpus Christi, Tex.: Life Seminars, 1980.

Neall, Ralph E. "The Nearness and the Delay of the Parousia in the Writings of Ellen G. White." Ph.D. dissertation, Andrews University, 1982.

Olson, Robert. "Outline Studies on Christian Perfection and Original Sin." *Ministry* Supplement, October 1970.

Poirier, Tim. "A Comparison of the Christology of Ellen White and Henry Melvill." Shelf Document. Washington, D.C.: Ellen G. White Estate, 1982.

Schwarz, Richard. *Light Bearers to the Remnant.* Mountain View, Calif.: Pacific Press Pub. Assn., 1979.

Seventh-day Adventists Answer Questions on Doctrine. Washington, D.C.: Review and Herald Pub. Assn., 1957.

Steinweg, Virginia. *Without Fear of Favor: The Life of M. L. Andreasen.* Washington, D.C.: Review and Herald Pub. Assn., 1979.

Wallenkampf, A. V., and W. Richard Lesher, eds. *The Sanctuary and the Atonement.* Washington, D.C.: Review and Herald Pub. Assn., 1981.

Webster, Eric C. *Crosscurrents in Adventist Christology.* New York: Peter Lang, 1984. Republished Berrien Springs, Mich.: Andrews University Press, 1992.

Wesley, John. *The Works of John Wesley.* Jackson ed. Peabody, Mass.: Hendrickson Pub., Inc., 1984. 14 vols.

_____. *The Works of John Wesley.* Albert Outler. Bicentennial ed. Nashville: Abingdon, 1984-1987. Vols. 1-4.

Whidden, Woodrow W. *Ellen White on Salvation: A Chronological Study.* Hagerstown, Md.: Review and Herald Pub. Assn., 1995.

_____. "Essential Adventism or Historic Adventism?" *Ministry,* October 1993.

_____. "The Humanity of Christ, Perfection, and the Vindication of God: What About 'The Harvest Principle' and 'The Final Generation'?" *Ministry,* October 1994.

_____. "The Soteriology of Ellen G. White: The Persistent Path to Perfection, 1836-1902." Ph.D dissertation, Drew University, 1989.

Wieland, R. J. *An Introduction to the 1888 Message Itself.* Baker, Oreg.: Adventist Forum Association, 1976.

_____. *The 1888 Message: An Introduction.* Nashville: Southern Pub. Assn., 1980.

_____. *"The Golden Chain": Is There a Broken Link?* Paris, Ohio: 1888 Message Study Committee, 1995.